T0149386

SERVE to LEAD

TIM FANNING

WESTBOW
PRESS®
A DIVISION OF THOMAS NELSON
& ZONDERVAN

Scripture quotations are taken from the Holman Christian Standard Bible®, Copyright © 1999, 2000, 2002, 2003, 2009 by Holman Bible Publishers. Used by permission. Holman Christian Standard Bible®, Holman CSB®, and HCSB® are federally registered trademarks of Holman Bible Publishers.

WestBow Press books may be ordered through booksellers or by contacting:

WestBow Press
A Division of Thomas Nelson & Zondervan
1663 Liberty Drive
Bloomington, IN 47403
www.westbowpress.com
1 (866) 928-1240

Because of the dynamic nature of the Internet, any web addresses or links contained in this book may have changed since publication and may no longer be valid. The views expressed in this work are solely those of the author and do not necessarily reflect the views of the publisher, and the publisher hereby disclaims any responsibility for them.

Any people depicted in stock imagery provided by Thinkstock are models, and such images are being used for illustrative purposes only. Certain stock imagery © Thinkstock.

ISBN: 978-1-5127-7519-8 (sc)
ISBN: 978-1-5127-7520-4 (hc)
ISBN: 978-1-5127-7518-1 (e)

Library of Congress Control Number: 2017902127

Print information available on the last page.

WestBow Press rev. date: 02/16/2017

"Tim – thank you for sharing God's path for your life with the world. What a great motivation for those who want to make a difference and are looking for a purpose. Tim's journey reminds us of the influential people in our lives and how impactful small acts of kindness can have on people we interact with daily. I personally picked up lessons throughout to share and enjoyed hearing how God has worked through Tim as a coach, father, husband and missionary. SERVE TO LEAD has refocused my intention to be a better servant and more yielding to God's perfect plan." *Butch Thompson, Auburn University, Head Baseball Coach*

I would like to dedicate this book to my mother, Mary Lee Fountain. She has always been my inspiration to persevere through any struggle in life and has been my biggest fan, regardless of success or failure. I love you, Mom!

Contents

SERVE TO LEAD

INTRODUCTION

I think more often than not, when we search for answers to life's little mysteries, we are looking in the wrong places. We seek insight from famous people, television shows, or radio personalities. Don't get me wrong; there are inspirational bursts from all of these places. People rise from poverty, personal tragedy, or disabilities to achieve great success, and all of a sudden, their stardom makes us pay attention. Were they not the same people before they were famous? My point is that we are surrounded by these people every day, and for some reason, we don't see them.

The fact of the matter is just about everything that I have built my life on was so graciously given to me by people you've never heard of, and I would venture to say you never will. We are so consumed with what we are fed on social and mainstream media, we fail to realize we are walking in fields of gold every day; we are surrounded by nuggets of life that can sustain us for all our days. All we have to do is pay attention, and the blueprint is there to follow. What am I taking about? I am talking about servants! They will teach us all we need to know, and there will be plenty leftover to teach others.

Sometimes these people are hard to see because they don't want to be seen. They operate behind the scenes, with no fanfare or any desire to be recognized. A single mother who works three jobs and never buys anything for herself. A Little League coach who buys cleats and a glove for one of his players without anyone knowing. A co-worker who stops to ask you about your family when he or she is up against a project deadline at work. A bus driver who greets every kid with a smile regardless of what's going on in his or her life. A coach who stays after practice to talk to one of his or her players about life despite his or her partner and children waiting at home. The socially awkward kid who finds the courage to tell the starting quarterback he really enjoyed watching him play on Friday night. Of course, the soldier who straps his boots on every day with no hesitation and provides the very freedom for us that we many times take for granted.

The list of examples could go on forever, but I think you get the point. All these people serve others, and in return, they expect nothing! People seem to be starving for inspiration, and all they have to do is look around. No, it's not sexy, but it's the very foundation for a life that has meaning. Serving others plants seeds in countless lives, and when watered, it often produces leaders without us even knowing. Over the course of this book, I will share what I have experienced while serving others, give examples of remarkable selflessness from people all over the world, and attempt to give thanks to so many who have poured themselves into me without ever asking for anything in return. My goal is to inspire people to embrace putting others ahead of themselves and let them know that by doing this, their lives will have a much greater purpose. In turn, they can empower others to achieve more than they ever imagined possible!

CHAPTER 1

Life of Service

A life of service is anything but easy, and it requires constant sacrifice. It is also hard to identify sometimes, simply because the results are often miles or even years away. The forks in the road are so often very similar in appearance, and it becomes hard to choose which one to take. Therefore, service requires faith! Faith is exactly that, and it requires us to open our hearts and minds to some things that may be uncomfortable at times but extremely necessary. If we knew the results, it wouldn't require us to step out of our comfort zone and show complete vulnerability.

Not everyone believes they are being called to a life of service, but if we are believers in Jesus Christ, it is the life he has blessed us with. Serving others doesn't have to be flashy, and most often, it only involves investing our time and opening our hearts. Our eyes are blinded to these opportunities quite frequently because we are looking to move on as quickly as possible. In our fast-paced society, there is always something else on the to-do list.

Many of us work fifty, sixty, or even seventy hours a week. How many times have you heard someone say that there are not enough hours in a day? A lot, I would imagine. We hear it all the time because it runs through everyone's brain. I know many times as I reflect on the day late at night, I ask myself, *Did I miss an opportunity to invest in someone other than myself today?* Often, the answer is yes.

Unfortunately, we cannot go back and say, "Good morning," to that person we walked right by or just go back and ask the person how his or her day is going. If you never ask, there is no opportunity to shed the smallest ray of light into the life of a person who may desperately need it. So many times, we walk around in our little bubble and never open our eyes to see what is going on. You have no idea if someone is in an abusive relationship, just lost a loved one, is fighting an addiction, or is simply struggling with his or her spirituality. To be a positive influence for someone battling those things, it takes an investment of time.

Teachers and coaches have the greatest opportunity to be servants, and this is simply because they have a captive audience for about eight hours a day—and when it comes to coaches, sometimes it's twelve hours a day. What better platform can there be when young men and women are being shaped and molded into the people they will become for the rest of their lives? Dr. Billy Graham was quoted as saying, "One coach will impact more young people in one year than the average person does in a lifetime."

It is an enormous responsibility with big consequences but with even greater rewards! Look at the first true teacher ever to walk the face of the earth: Jesus. He led by example every day. He poured himself into others so they would, in turn, do the same. He knew his days were numbered, so he paid the ultimate sacrifice and served until his last breath. Over two thousand years later, his service inspires, comforts, and leaves an unshakeable example to follow.

Not everyone will choose a career that involves teaching and coaching young men and women. The United States Armed Forces are as good an example of serving something bigger than yourself as you can find in the world today. These professions are vitally important to the moral fabric of our society, but it is so important to understand that anyone can lead a life of service.

I had a Little League coach who invested so much in me, and I only hope he feels rewarded by the man I strive to be every day. I grew up without a father, so he was the first male role model I had when I could understand what that meant. He had a huge effect on my life, and his actions allowed me to see that there were people willing to help with no strings attached. There was only one reason for this grace he showed to me: he had a servant's heart! There are youth coaches all over the country who provide this type of leadership on a daily basis. Most often, they do not realize the positive influence of their actions until many years later.

What if Jesus had sat on the sidelines? He could have watched as men and women morally destroyed themselves, but he didn't. He chose a life of service, and we should be eternally grateful. Yes, his act of service to humankind is unmatched, but his everyday acts of kindness give us a blueprint for serving others. I have seen firsthand the effect that Habitat for Humanity can have on a family's life. Volunteering at a soup kitchen, at a battered women's shelter, or at your church, or even just donating clothes to Goodwill are all great opportunities to help. There are countless organizations that can and will always need help.

I would recommend that everyone, at some point in time, if physically able, should go on a mission trip. It will change your life forever. If for nothing else, it will give you a greater appreciation for the life God has blessed you with. It's not possible to give that much of yourself and not feel its effects immediately. Remember though, putting a smile on someone's face at a homeless shelter for even the briefest of moments may make all the difference in the world. Hammering those nails on a roof that provides safety and shelter to someone who has experienced only personal tragedy can change a person's life forever. That's what servants do. Philippians 2:3-4 tells us, "Do nothing out of rivalry or conceit, but in humility consider others as more important than yourselves. Everyone should look out not only for his own interests but also for the interests of others" (Holman Christian Standard Bible).

This holds true on a daily basis at work as well. If you have been blessed with a position of leadership, it is imperative that those looking to you for guidance and leadership see servant qualities. The most influential leaders over the course of time have inspired people through leading a life of service: Mother Teresa, Gandhi, and Martin Luther King Jr. Leading with fear or a strong-armed approach will only last so long because, eventually, those who work for you see it as exactly that. They should feel as though they are working with you instead of for you. They may begin to have no reservations about clocking out as quickly as possible without being penalized. However, if they feel you are emotionally invested in them as individuals and that you treat them with respect, they will follow you anywhere. This takes an investment of time. A servant-leader has no problem getting to know employees' families, their likes and dislikes, their favorite sports teams, where they attend church, or if they like to travel. This means it is about serving something bigger than yourself and not the bottom line. The goal of every leader should be to build other great leaders. You should lead employees as if they would eventually take your job. Leaders that only use fear and scare tactics are often masking insecurities about their personal lives, professions, or spirituality.

This holds true in education, military service, manufacturing, or raising a family. Being the leader of your family is more important than any job title you could possibly obtain. Children love unconditionally, and it slowly slips as the world weighs on them. They are blinded by expectations, not only from their peers but also by their parents. Take them with you when volunteering. Let them see the influence one person or a group of people can have on the world. If children are shown examples of kindness by serving others, there is a good chance that as they grow and mature, they too will choose this path because it is already ingrained in them. Today, so many of us find ourselves worrying about how much money we earn, how big our houses are, or how good our clothes look. I am going to let you in on a little secret: we can't take any of those things with us! I once heard Denzel Washington say during a speech, "I have never seen a U-Haul attached to a hearse!" The only thing we have with us as we stand before God is our salvation. What have we done to further his kingdom on earth? Have we given to others as his son has given to us?

CHAPTER 2

Self-Pity

"I never saw a wild thing feel sorry for itself. A bird will fall frozen dead from a bow, never having felt sorry for itself." Those words from D.H. Lawrence have always resonated with me. It is a very natural occurrence for people to feel sorry for themselves. We have all been there before. It is all too easy to blame someone else for our own shortcomings.

> I wish I had grown up with money; then things would be different!
>
> I wish my parents hadn't gotten divorced; then things would be different!
>
> If my coach would just give me a chance to play, then things would be different!
>
> I wish my boss could see my potential; then things would be different!
>
> If he or she would just go out on a date with me, then things would be different!
>
> If my parents had taken me to church as a kid, then things would be different!

The list could go on and on, but I think you get the picture. We seem to live in a world of excuses instead of solutions! It amazes me the number of people I see walking with their heads down on a daily basis. If people would just look up and see the world that is right in front of them, there is no telling what they could accomplish. God puts so many wonderful opportunities in front of each and every one us; we just have to open our eyes. No one determines your fate and your ability to contribute to this world as a servant but you! It is essential that we all identify our strengths and weaknesses by being honest with ourselves. This allows us the ability to deal with failure in a more positive manner and not hide from it by feeling sorry for ourselves. "The essence of man is imperfection," said Norman Cousins. An inability to do this can lead to depression, anger issues at home, a lack of professional focus, obesity, alcoholism, and even wavering in your spirituality. If we were all perfect, then what could anyone possibly have to offer us? How could anyone invest in us as people if we had it all figured out already?

Self-pity affects kids, young adults, working professionals, and the elderly. No one, regardless of age, is immune to the self-pity disease. For example, most kids today are told all too often how good they are. Therefore, when they begin to fail at things—and they will, because everyone does at some point— they don't have the mental toughness to handle the situation. That's why it's extremely important for parents to prepare their children for when they aren't the superstar. We are so afraid of our children's own failures that we can cripple them for life by shielding them from it. We should, as parents, point out positive contributions to the team and not strictly focus on the individual accomplishments. Eventually, it will have to be a team effort for them to be successful, regardless of what profession they choose as adults.

Through years of experience, I have noticed that the best player in youth sports is very rarely the best player in high school. Of course, there are exceptions, but most of them have gone through puberty before most of their teammates and haven't really had to work very hard to be the best. As they get older, many of those kids catch up physically and even pass the superstar because they had to develop the work ethic to stay competitive. On top of that, it seems like this generation of parents live through their children and place such high expectations on them, it ends up burning kids out. Unfortunately, instead of working to remain one of the best players, they give up on the sport altogether and sometimes even resent their parents as a result. If we as parents are not able to accept our kids' mistakes, how will they ever learn to cope with them? Hall of Fame coach Rick Pitino was quoted as saying, "Failure is good; it's fertilizer. Everything I've learned about coaching, I've learned from making mistakes."

Young adults may experience self-pity while in college or as they prepare to enter the professional world. Most often in college, these problems surface in large part because of time-management issues. Many are away from their parents for the first time and have so much free time that they struggle; in high school, almost every day is mapped out for them, right up until it's time for bed. Therefore, young adults are not usually disciplined enough to handle all of their extracurricular activities, on top of a full class load, until they figure out there is time for everything they want to do. So when they start doing poorly on tests and oversleeping for early classes, and their love lives are not going according to plan, you can bet that late at night alone in their dorm rooms, there are a lot of pity parties. Students that have jobs and/or play collegiate athletics have a little more success with time management because of a lack of free time, but it is a struggle all the same.

When they get out of college or choose a profession without a degree, this begins what everyone calls the *real world*. How many times have you said this to your kids: "Wait until you get into the real world?" If you haven't yet, trust me ... you will. We all have visions and aspirations of the first job we are going to have. We are going to take the world by storm. As mature adults, we know for the most part that this is not reality. Sometimes it takes people a lifetime to find a dream job where they feel they truly are making difference, and unfortunately it may never happen. So what do we do then ... feel sorry for ourselves? I love what John Maxwell says in his book, *Failing Forward*, "The difference between average people and achieving people is their perception of and response to failure."

Self-pity is less prevalent in middle-age professionals because most are in the midst of chasing a pot of gold at the end of the rainbow (also known as the corporate ladder). Most are also busy taking their kids back and forth to athletic events, dance recitals, or private lessons of some kind. It doesn't leave much time for self-pity—only sleep! However, this part of life is when many people begin to have regrets. "I should have done this (skydiving, hang gliding, rock climbing, surfing, etc.) before I had kids. Man, I didn't know having a family would be this expensive, and I can't travel as much because of our children's commitments." We have all said or thought this at some point in time: "I just wish I could do what I want to do for a change." With each passing birthday, these feelings are much harder to ignore. As Billy Crystal said in *City Slickers*, "Do you ever wake up and say to yourself, Is this the best I'm ever gonna look, the best I'm ever gonna to feel, and it ain't that great?"

The truth of the matter is that we all share the same experiences in some way, shape, or form. It's how we choose to deal with them as individuals that is sometimes completely different. We must not allow the negative thoughts to overcome the obvious blessings. Be inclusive when it comes to your family and truly invest in them, and those pity parties will fade away. I am certainly not telling you to hurl your child out of an airplane or hang them off a rock face, but go hiking with them, have them volunteer with you on community service projects, take them on trips when possible, and just spend time with them that you will never have again. What this also does is build a family structure that will be repeated when your children become parents of their own.

As people enter their golden years, they struggle with feeling relevant. They are on the backside of their careers, and the younger versions of themselves seems a distant memory. Everyone seems to know more about technology, drives faster than they do, and has a much better solution to all the world's problems. In retirement especially, the days seem to last longer, become very irrelevant, and are certainly less fulfilling. It is essential as we grow older that we find a way to invest in others so that we find purpose in every day we are blessed with. No matter how much money we make, professional awards we accumulate, or exotic places we visit, nothing we fill our cup and sustain us more when it matters most than serving others. We can all justify our feelings of self-pity no matter what walk of life we currently reside in, but the only way to truly prevent it is by serving something greater than ourselves.

When I speak to groups, more often than not, self-pity is the main topic of discussion. I believe it's one of the biggest problems crippling our country today. We have enabled and spoiled our children to the point that it sometimes makes it difficult for them to stand on their own two feet. We shield them from failure, and everything always seems to be someone else's fault. Why does it have to be someone else's fault? Maybe things happen for a reason. Failure is how we learn to live!

Doctor visits have become the norm instead of being saved for emergencies. As a teacher, I see it on a daily basis, and as an athletic director, I have begun to see it professionally with this generation. Kids miss more days of school, and teachers seem to find it easier to call in sick. How can I preach to my players about pushing through adversity if I am not willing to do the same? It ties directly into that level of commitment we expect from them on a daily basis on the field and in the classroom. If we show kids they can perform when everything is not optimal, there is a good chance they will apply that to their professional life.

I have missed two days in eighteen years as a teacher. One was for an appendectomy and the other for the birth of one of my daughters. So do you think I haven't been sick during all that time? Therefore at my house, the rule is, "If I go to school, they go to school." In thirteen years, my eldest daughter has missed school once, and in eleven years, my youngest daughter has missed once. Do you think in all that time, they haven't been sick?

We used to call that "tough love" when I was growing up. Now when people use that term, this generation freaks out and parents are seen as abusive. It really has nothing to do with spanking children, although I do not have a problem with that when necessary. But it has everything to do with raising children who have a legitimate chance to impact the world in a positive manner. In my opinion, it's what we are sorely lacking in today's society. I have found my own definition of tough love, and I call it "raw love!"

R – Respect: not only respect for parents, grandparents, and teachers, but for everyone you come in contact with, regardless of like, dislikes, gender, race, creed, or religion.

A – Accountability: be there when you are supposed to be and even when you don't have to be.

W – Work Ethic: it takes no talent to give effort, and eventually you will be successful if you just refuse to give up.

L – Leadership: let them see you lead by serving others, and put them in uncomfortable situations where they have to do the same.

O – Obedience: not only to parents, elders, and bosses, but to God's path for their lives.

V – Vulnerability: show them it's okay to let your guard down and truly pour your heart out; it's the only way to find true love, friendships and have a personal relationship with Jesus Christ.

E – Education: always strive to learn, not just in school, but about yourself, in your profession, and about your faith.

Raising children is probably the hardest thing in the world to do, and at the same time, the most rewarding. No one gets it right all the time, certainly not me, but I do think if we all apply a little raw love, the results will be noticeable and significant in the long run. I can promise you this: self-pity is not an option if we wish to leave this world better than we found it.

CHAPTER 3

God's Path

I think most children grow up and think they are destined for greatness at some point. Everyone wants to be a superstar, right? So what does that mean? Well if we watch television, that probably means a professional athlete, actor, politician, or CEO of a Fortune 500 company. That couldn't be further from the truth. We think these things signify greatness because that's what society tells us. Very seldom do you see a janitor on television who has worked for thirty years at the same school and changed countless lives during that time, simply because he always put the kids before himself. He merely shared a kind word when he showed up to work before anyone else or stayed after everyone else had gone home for the evening. That lonely kid sitting on the sidewalk only needed an investment of time to make all the difference in the world. Maybe that janitor is the example that kid needed to show him or her accountability, kindness, and that it doesn't matter what the time clock says. God has a path for all of us. Maybe that path is that of a professional athlete, a lawyer, a doctor, or a mechanic; it is really irrelevant.

Quite frankly, most times that path is hard to see. There are many twists, turns, peaks, and valleys, but rest assured, it is right there in front of you. It takes prayer and a lot of faith. But faith, in itself, is difficult for many of us because we want the answers to the test. One of my favorite lines in a movie is by Tom Hanks in *A League of Their Own*. His star player is about to quit the team because it just got too hard, and his response is, "If it wasn't hard, everyone would do it. The hard is what makes it great!" The same is true during our walk on God's path; the decisions are often difficult because we don't see the results immediately.

I would encourage everyone to do an exercise as you read this. Take a piece of paper and begin to write a chronological diagram of your path so far in life—starting from where you were born and ending where you currently reside today. In between those points, begin to fill in your stops along the way. This would include, but is not limited to, college choices, jobs you have taken, churches you have attended, or even how you met your significant other. There are no limits to this; include as much as you want because you will be blown away by what you find. Some of the smallest details in your life, God put there; and some would define these as "divine appointments." As you think about these significant milestones in your life, reflect back and ask what nudged you one way or the other. "Why did I choose this direction instead of another? Did I pray when making these decisions? Whom did I seek advice from during this time?" As a child, these paths are most often determined by our parents, but their decisions are extremely influential in our decision-making process as we get older. Parents are the first examples we have. Their lives unfold right in front of us, and we steadily catalog these things in our minds, even if we do it unknowingly. Teachers, coaches, pastors, or even older siblings are more examples of influential people who help us shape our perspective while we choose a path in life. One of the greatest gifts God bestowed upon us is the power of choice!

As I have asked each of you to examine God's path for your life, I will do the same. My mother was born in Foxboro, Massachusetts. She chose a life of service by enlisting in the United States Army to be a nurse, which led her to be stationed in Fort Benning, Georgia. Shortly thereafter, she had me out of wedlock and decided to keep me instead of giving me up for adoption. This meant she would be discharged. This was not a popular decision with her family, so we settled in Columbus, Georgia, which was just outside the base. Until I was nine, we lived in South Columbus, and then we moved to East Columbus, across from Eastern Little League and the Boy's Club. As I look back, I know God led my mother here. That Little League coach I mentioned earlier, Coach Gary—this is where our paths crossed. It was my first experience with organized sports, and it was definitely what I needed to keep me focused and out of trouble. Not to mention I had access to the Boy's Club every day after school; it was a blessing for a single mother not to have to worry where I was. This was also about the same time we changed churches and I began to develop a personal relationship with Christ. Several years later, as high school was quickly approaching, my mother moved us to North Columbus, where I attended Jordan High School.

In high school, my paths crossed with Coach Fred Maynard and Coach Paul Waldrop. Coach Maynard was young and just out of college. He treated me like a little brother, which included kicking me in the butt on occasion to keep me on the straight and narrow in the classroom. He really invested time in me when he wasn't on the clock, which included after-school pick-up basketball games and just talking about life in general. I can still see those rec-specs he wore like it was yesterday. Coach Waldrop was a seasoned veteran and really challenged me as an athlete. He made me realize that playing college athletics was a realistic goal. He was a disciplinarian in every sense of the word and held everyone accountable for their actions. Not to mention he bought me my letterman jacket because my mother couldn't afford one. How would my life have turned out if these men hadn't chosen a life of service? I decided to attend Berry College on a baseball scholarship. The decision wasn't easy, but I felt its academic reputation and beautiful campus in the North Georgia Mountains put it over the top for me.

After only one semester in college, I found myself at a crossroads. The coach who recruited me was leaving to take another job, and I just felt like I was being led in another direction. I had friends from high school playing baseball at Middle Georgia College in Cochran, Georgia. Like the reputation Berry College built academically, MGC had built a reputation for nationally ranked junior college teams and producing professional baseball players. So how would I get there? Well, I didn't have a car, so I had to talk a teammate into taking me three hours south; and even then, I had no idea if the legendary Coach Robert Sapp would even take me. I showed up, glove in hand, and asked for a tryout. I don't know if he saw something in me or just felt sorry for me, but I know God had a plan. What do you know—the friends I knew from high school left before I started the next semester.

Almost a year after I made that big decision, as I was eating in the cafeteria, in walked my future wife. I chased her down the hall like a stalker, and the rest, as they say, is history. That was twenty-four years ago, and we have two beautiful daughters because of it. What is unfortunate is that so many people will say,

"Man, that is ironic." There is nothing ironic about it; God's path put me in that exact place at that exact time, and he gave me the strength to act. How many times in life do we want to go back in time and try to play Monday morning quarterback? That only leads to the biggest regrets in our lives. I could have just as easily become stricken with the fear of rejection, but that's what faith is all about! Six months later, I was faced with another life-altering decision on where to go after junior college.

I was so blessed to have several scholarship offers to great four-year schools, but up until this point in my life, it was definitely the most difficult decision, by far. On paper, it seemed like an easy decision to stay closer to home, but in the end, I chose Marshall University, which geographically made the least amount of sense, being over eight hours away. When I visited, something in my gut felt right even though I knew it would put a tremendous strain on my relationship with Renee and I would only get to come home twice a year. It was extremely hard in many ways, but I would find out years later why God's path led me there.

After I was done playing college baseball, I signed a two-year, independent minor league contract to play for the Portsmouth Explorers of the Frontier League. During the off-season, I got a job at Neil's Sports Shop and took a few classes to finish up my degree. Not long after, another big decision in my life was about to unfold. I was given the opportunity to travel around the entire country for three months with the Olympic Torch Relay. The company I was working for had secured the merchandising rights and was putting together a team to do mobile merchandise that started in Los Angeles and would finish in Atlanta for the start of the 1996 Olympic Games. So what was God's path? If I took this opportunity, it was almost certain my baseball career would be over, not to mention I would be away from my fiancée for three months. Over the past four years, we had been apart nearly half the time, but after weighing the options, I decided to go. As I look back on this part of my life, sometimes I wonder, if I had to do it all over again, would I make the same decision? All of our lives are filled with these moments, and that is why faith is such an integral part of the path we choose.

It really was the experience of a lifetime up until that point in my life. I had never traveled anywhere baseball had not taken me, so seeing so much beauty really opened my eyes to a world I didn't know existed. From flower farms in the Pacific Northwest to the breathtaking Rocky Mountains; the start of the Mississippi River in Minnesota to where it ends in New Orleans; the beginning of the Erie Canal and Niagara Falls to the swamps of South Florida. Of course, I also didn't mind meeting Rick Pitino in Louisville and Bill Russell in Seattle or getting to run the Olympic torch close to my hometown as my mom looked on. But only until after this wonderful experience was over did I truly understand why this path was there for me. The company I was working for offered me a full-time job, and that allowed me to close the baseball chapter of my life and legitimately look toward marriage.

Over the next three years, I would travel all over the world, managing merchandise venues at sporting events. We went to Japan for the Winter Olympics, France for World Cup Soccer, worked two Super Bowls, and did all the SEC and Big East Championship games. I was in my early twenties, standing on the sidelines of an SEC Football Championship game, sitting in the first row in Madison Square Garden for the Big East Championship Game right behind legendary Syracuse coach Jim Boeheim, and I even got to meet Muhammad Ali at an event we did. What a blessing. It was high intensity, with constant problem solving. I was around some of the biggest sporting events in the world. It helped fill a void in my life now that college athletics were a thing of the past. Renee and I were married in May of 1997, and my trip to Japan was in January of 1998. It was tough going away for almost a month as a newlywed, but wouldn't you know, the first person who walked in our venue when we opened the doors was someone I knew from the torch relay. Now that's a divine appointment! Our lives are littered with God's subtle touches like that, knowing what we need and when we need it.

Little did I know that around the corner would be a life-changing decision. The company I was working for bought back the Game Headwear Company, and my job responsibilities changed. After a while in my new assignment, I knew deep down in my heart that this was not my calling. When you go from a position that's so fast-paced and constantly changes at the drop of a hat to a more traditional nine-to-five environment, it shocks the system. I was used to working one-hundred-hour workweeks at an event and traveling to places I had never been before, and the electricity that accompanied special events was hard to replace. It was a great company, and my bosses were great people. They had given me the opportunity to travel around the world, and in a lot of ways helped shape my perspective on life. Again, several years later I would understand exactly why God allowed me this opportunity and how important it would be to his path for the rest of my life.

As I began searching for answers on pretty much a daily basis, a friend of mine called me about a teaching and coaching position at Glenwood School. Glenwood is a small private school in Phenix City, Alabama. I grew up in public school education; however, during high school, I had friends from summer baseball that went to school there, so I had heard about it. After discussing it with my wife, I went for an interview and realized very quickly it was a something I wanted to do. Now wanting to do something and having the courage to actually do it are two very different things entirely. First, I had to go home and tell my wife what the contract offer was and that it would be a significant pay cut. Second, she was right in the middle of getting her Masters of Physical Therapy at the Medical College of Georgia, which was being done at a satellite campus an hour and half away from where we lived. Third, there would be a lot of ramen noodles on the menu until she graduated.

Of course, Renee has always supported everything I have ever done, so the newest chapter of my life had begun. Not only was our headmaster a great leader, I also had the privilege of working for two of the greatest coaches in Alabama history. Our football coach, Wayne Trawick, is the second winningest coach in Alabama high school history and our basketball coach/athletic director, Doug Key, is the second winningest coach in Alabama Junior College history. They have been elected to numerous halls of fame, and these are the men who God placed in my life to spend time with on a daily basis. The first two things I noticed was how humble they were and how they treated everyone. They have no idea what an impact that made on me as a young man searching for inspiration.

It wasn't very long into my coaching career when I knew I could make a difference in the lives of young men and women. Earlier in this chapter when I said it would be years later before I realized why I ended up at Marshall University, well here you go. Three years into coaching, one of my former players, Josh

McConnell, was playing baseball at Faulkner University, and he called to tell me it wasn't working out. He was done with baseball. My response was, "No, you're not; you are about to get in this truck with me and take a journey." I was getting ready to take two kids up to Marshall (eight and a half hours away) for a camp. And wouldn't you know, he ended playing Division I baseball for three years because of my relationship with that program. He even ended up going to Spain to play baseball. How cool is that? Josh also came back home after he was finished with school and has coached with me for nine years. He chose to invest in others the same way people had invested in him. It gets better, as I will soon explain. I want to stay chronologically on God's path in my life for the sake of this chapter.

After four years of being an assistant coach in baseball, basketball, and football, I was given the opportunity to be the head baseball coach in the spring of 2004 and athletic director in 2005. I only tell you this because choices needed to be made on how to run a baseball program, and when there are choices to be made, God's path comes into play. The Glenwood baseball program is steeped in tradition; they had won fourteen state championships in thirty-four years of existence, but had not won a title since 1993. That just happened to coincide with long-time and celebrated Major Leaguer Tim Hudson's graduation. I had a vision, and it required a lot of changes. Usually with change comes resistance, and wouldn't you know, two of my former bosses at my previous job had become two of my biggest supporters. Phil Stillwell was a co-founder of the Game Headwear Company, and Tommy Allison was a partner in their current business, and both of their sons played for me. Even though you know what you're doing is right, sometimes you still need that support system for encouragement when self-doubt creeps in. You need someone to say, "Stay the course!" They are still two of my very best friends to this day. You think God put them on my path for a reason?

I feel the next significant road on God's path for me started in about 2011. We had just won a third consecutive state championship, but I just felt more was needed from me as a servant. Mrs. Lynda Wright, a science teacher at our school, had been taking groups to Central America for about fifteen years for summer service trips. I would always talk to her about these trips when they returned, and quite frankly, I was very envious of their experiences. We would talk about how I needed to take my players and teach kids baseball. Well, that summer when they returned, Mrs. Wright told me she found the perfect place for us to start. Again, it is one thing to talk about something and something entirely different stepping up to the plate and doing it. I started praying about this a lot and sharing my thoughts with Coach McConnell. He suggested that I call Marshall Murray, his best friend from college. Marshall had started a non-profit organization called More Than A Game. I met Marshall through Josh when they played together. Funny how Marshall University keeps popping up after a decision I made almost twenty years ago, but that's how God's path works. More Than A Game sponsored amateur teams in Northern California, with an emphasis on serving their community through camps, equipment drives, and local service projects. After talking with Marshall, I began to work on the blueprint for the international mission's side of More Than A Game. In October of 2012, we took our first trip to the village of Bongo in the northern province of Panama. Since then, we have been back to Panama, Cameroon (Africa), Colombia (South

America), and the Dominican Republic, and have done amazing things domestically as well.

I always felt drawn to a life of service, but as you make your way through life, sometimes the corporate ladder seems more attractive. Well like a lot of people, you don't realize how long that ladder is and what you may have to give up to reach the top. What I hope for everyone is that they don't look back twenty years from now and say, "What could I have done differently?" So you have to decide, is that God's path or is it your path?

CHAPTER 4

Panama

For the most part, people want to be good. I bet if you ask one hundred people, ninety-five of them would tell you that they always wanted to go on a mission trip but just never have. When the opportunity arose and the invitation was extended, suddenly the laundry list of reasons why they couldn't go started piling up: finances, work, kids, illness, lack of travel experience, fear of traveling to the region. This is very common when anyone attempts to step out of their comfort zone. It is natural for us to second guess, rationalize, and experience fear when it comes to matters of the heart. If you can ever overcome that fear and merely just give your heart a chance, it will allow your hands to touch so many. I have personally witnessed the transformation in people when they just let go and commit. The only way I know how to explain it is that it's like watching the curtain rise at a play and seeing a whole new world you never noticed before. Then you start thinking, *This has been right in front of me, and I have never taken a moment to open my eyes and see it.* It's so fulfilling to watch people experience this because it is truly life-changing. Colors are brighter, sounds are sharper, and even smells are more magnified. As the old saying goes, "It's like a kid in a candy store!"

This is a good opportunity to tell you about the aforementioned mission trips and the impact they have had, not only on my life, but countless others. The thing about organizing mission trips is that you can prepare all you want and do all the research your brain can handle, but the reality is that when you have boots on the ground you have to expect the unexpected! Prepare to be disappointed at times and at the same time have your heart melt like butter. One thing I have learned, without a shadow of a doubt, is to never expect to be on time! It is extremely hard for us to comprehend this because the society we live in is totally built on schedules. A lot of our lives revolve around being at work at a certain time, taking a lunch break at a certain time, or being at an event at a certain time. In most countries, that is abnormal instead of the norm. Everything moves at a much slower pace, and the sooner you come to grips with that, the more you can accomplish and, better yet, appreciate it.

Our first trip was to Bongo, Panama. It is located about twenty miles from the border of Costa Rica at the base of Volcan Baru. We flew into Panama City, spent the night in a hotel, and were up at 4:00 a.m. to catch a small commuter plane to David, Panama. Seeing the expressions on the kids' faces when that plane taxied in with twin-engine propellers was priceless. It probably didn't help the anxiety level very much when, at the ticket counter, the attendant asked everyone their weight. One of the best things about stepping out of your comfort zone is being able to share all these once-in-a-lifetime experiences with others. We were the last people to get on the plane because I wanted to get video of everyone getting on together; and we soon realized that having a seat assignment on your ticket didn't really mean anything. The flight was completely full, so we took the only seats available. I was the very last person to get on, and just as we discussed earlier, God's path was laid out for me. This time it was about four feet wide and had running lights directly to where I was supposed to be at that moment in my life. I sat down next to an older gentleman. He looked like he was straight out of a Panama Jack commercial: tan, with white linen pants, a black silk shirt, and a white hat. His name was Frank Melgar, and he just fell in love with our kids and was so appreciative of the mission we were on. He was very adamant about helping us with any future trips we wanted to take involving the kids of Panama. I would later learn just how serious he was about that proposition.

After we landed, white knuckles and all, it was time to rent our van and begin a rather tedious thirty-minute drive that turned into two and half hours. Little did we know that on this day, there would be protestors blocking the main road to our destination, so it was "figure it out" mode. But like always, God knew what he had planned for us because our journey was through some of the most beautiful countryside I have ever seen. When we finally turned onto that gravel road, it was like going through a portal to another dimension. We had to cross a one-lane bridge over this gorgeous river, and when I saw a man riding on a horse, I figured it would be different than what we were used to. We stayed with a retired Methodist minister, Secundino Morales, and his wife, Vicky. It seemed like every inch of this village was covered with some sort of crop. The air was filled with the smell of citrus because everywhere you walked, there were oranges and limes just lying on the ground. Our goal was to work with two small schools in the village on basic baseball fundamentals, supply them with equipment and uniforms, and also leave them FCA Bibles printed in Spanish. After talking with Secundino, we learned that two elderly people in the village needed vegetable gardens built, so we immediately added that to the list of priorities.

While surveying the village, we quickly realized that finding somewhere flat to do a baseball clinic was impossible, so we used a small piece of uneven, rocky land in front of one of the schools until we could come up with an alternative solution. So we broke out all the bat bags full of equipment and set up a throwing, fielding, and even a hitting station up against an old hog-wire fence. It really didn't matter where we were; all that mattered was that every boy and girl had a smile on their face. During the hitting station, one of the boys hit the ball into the jungle and came back with an orange instead. Well, they decided to hit that too! In the throwing station, one boy looked like he was pitching the seventh game of the World Series, he was so serious and focused. It was an amazing day. The next day, we found a field about twenty minutes away, but the problem was transporting everyone there. With Secundino's help, we had small pick-up trucks loaded with as many kids as possible. We had to use unpaved roads at very slow speeds, but eventually we were playing baseball in Concepcion. All the kids played in their school uniforms: boys in dress pants and the girls in dresses. Again, it didn't matter—all smiles! As soon as the trucks stopped, these kids sprinted to the field and were racing each other around the bases in 95-degree weather. Little things like this seemed to make a huge impact on our team. At home, it is easy to take for granted having a uniform, equipment, and a place to play. The kids from Bongo had none of these things. They walked jungle paths to school. Many of them lived on dirt floors. They ate to sustain life, not for self-satisfaction, and they were as happy as any kids I'd ever seen. The next day, we pulled out uniforms and hats to give all the kids; we might as well have been wearing Santa Claus outfits and passing out iPhones.

When we were done with baseball for the day, we bought all of the children drinks at the corner store. They were ice-cold glass bottles of peach, strawberry, apple, and orange soft drinks that cost forty cents each. After that, we worked on vegetable gardens each day. Of course, we had no idea what building a vegetable garden in Bongo, Panama, actually entailed, but it was interesting, to say the least. We did quickly figure out why we needed to do baseball in the mornings, because every afternoon the rain was definitely coming. At Daniel's house, we had to harvest bamboo and carry it about a mile through the jungle, and the only tool we had in the arsenal was a machete. It was definitely a more comprehensive job than we had anticipated, so it took about four afternoons to finish, but in the end, I think everyone was extremely proud of their work.

Each day after we finished, the team went for a refreshing swim in the local river; it was cold and crystal clear. It was a short hike after crawling under a fence, and it seemed as if we were transported to Jurassic Park. The river was surrounded by tall cliffs that were covered as far as the eye could see with massive ferns. The sun could barely break through the thick jungle canopy, so there were areas of beautiful shadows and very brief moments of sparkling sunlight off the rocky rapids. We did some rock surfing and even created our own spa, equipped with a homemade Jacuzzi created by the current from the top of the rocks. People back in the States spend several hundred dollars for this kind of relaxation therapy.

Another early morning started at 4:30 a.m. for our epic journey to the top of Vulcan Baru (eleven thousand and four hundred feet), the highest point in the country of Panama. We had about an hour drive before we started hiking. We met our two guides, Genover and Carlos, at the base of the volcano. I had heard stories of how hard this adventure would be, and in some opinions, it was an impossible task for a group this size. Altitude sickness and physical exhaustion were the two main concerns, but I believe it was that chance of impossibility that had our group so focused on making it. The hike started with dense jungle in the dark, so everyone had their headlamps on. It was like God created a stairway to heaven for us, despite how hard we could immediately tell it was going to be. Perfectly placed rocks and roots made steps attainable. It even seemed as if vines and branches were readily available upon request to use as ladders. After about two hours in the jungle, it began to clear a little and show more of the volcano's true nature. The next quadrant, as we called it, produced more rocks and narrow pathways. Each quadrant had slightly different vegetation, but each one as beautiful as the next.

Our guides were great about stopping for breaks, where we shared about the hike to that point, asked questions, and enjoyed some water or sandwiches made by Mrs. Morales. Each one of us had our own battle with the mountain. To the person, it was the hardest thing any of us had ever done. About six hours up, there were several of us questioning our judgment, but when we reached the summit, it was well worth it. I can't begin to explain how life-changing and freeing that experience was. There was also an eight-foot cross constructed at exactly eleven thousand and four hundred feet; there was a gold medallion put on it by the government to solidify its importance. It took us about seven hours to finally reach the top, so a little rest and meditation time was required.

We all spread out; some took a nap, some just stared out over the valley below, some enjoyed a little water, but I am quite sure all of us were processing random thoughts about what we had just accomplished. I took a moment by myself at the base of the cross to thank God for allowing me to be in that exact place in time and giving me the strength to do something so amazing. Before we began our trek down, I talked to the boys about what should follow by accomplishing a feat like this and that there is nothing in their lives too big for them to handle. This journey was only a microcosm of the obstacles they would surely face in life (God's path, school, marriage, kids, career, etc.).

We took a different route down the mountain and it was more in the shape of a very rocky road with ditches on both sides. After about ten total hours of hiking, everyone was out of water. We were not in dire straits by any means, but that sure didn't seem to matter because another divine appointment was just around the corner. It just so happens on this occasion it was with a two-liter bottle of water. As I was walking, I saw what I thought was a big bottle of water on the edge of the jungle. So I walked past it, back and forth, for a few seconds, maybe thinking I was on candid camera, but really thinking it might be booby trapped. After a few more seconds of deliberation, I picked it up and noticed it had never been opened before: unbelievable! I gathered everyone, we all shared, and certainly no one cared who they were drinking after.

It didn't take anyone very long to fall asleep that night. The next day, we were going to visit the schools and present them with the FCA Bibles and some school supplies that local college students from our area had donated. The end of this trip was quickly approaching, so everyone wanted to get one more swim in the river to put an exclamation point on our time in Bongo.

Little did we know it would be an adventure none of us would soon forget. It started off just like all the other days we went swimming. We were all spread out among the rapids in our little spas as we talked about the kids, Mrs. Morales's great food, hiking, and how we would explain this experience to our friends and family when we returned home. All of a sudden, we spotted a large log floating down the river. Not being from the mountains of Panama, it didn't seem that strange at first, but in about five minutes, we quickly realized what that floating log truly represented. Unbeknownst to us, it had been raining in the mountains all day, so the river was beginning to rise, and to say we were unprepared is an understatement. Within minutes, we were being overtaken by raging waters. Decisions had to be made immediately! There were five us at the bottom of the rapids who had a fighting chance if there was no hesitation, so we went for it. As the stronger swimmers made it to the bank, they extended large branches to give assistance.

However, there were four people trapped in the river up above, facing extreme decisions. I felt our best option for those guys was to stay put and work on a strategy for extraction. By this time, one young man lunged for the bank and crawled out through the jungle while the remaining three were above the water on large boulders. I didn't necessarily feel they would be swept away but amidst all this, darkness had fallen in the jungle. Cold, wet, pitch-black darkness and a raging river in the jungle is a pretty good recipe for high levels of anxiety. I sent two boys back to the house to get a rope as we made our way back upriver through some of the densest jungle I have ever seen. My goal while waiting for the rope to arrive was merely to calm any fears the guys may have had by just talking to them and letting them know what was going on. When the rope arrived, it wasn't heavy enough to throw across the water, so we tied a rock to the end to gain distance. Secundino had a flashlight behind me as I would make each toss and give me advice in his Panamanian James Earl Jones voice. Honestly, it felt like instructions from heaven because of the deep voice and rays of light bouncing off the trees. It took about another hour, but we finally were able to pull everyone out. It was definitely a trying moment and life lesson for all involved. When we finally made it back out to the road, with no shirts or shoes, huddled up together, we asked Secundino to say a prayer and thank God for his protection in our time of need. So there we stood, with no shirts, no shoes, soaking wet, shivering, holding hands, and standing in a circle, with only the headlights from the van illuminating a small area, giving thanks. It was truly a sight to see and certainly something I will never forget as long as I live.

Our next trip to Panama was certainly less eventful but every bit as challenging. During our first trip, we noticed the desire for playing the game of baseball was very real, but the kids didn't have a place to play. We had to take them some thirty minutes away to find a field, and for these families, that was unrealistic moving forward. Many of them did not have cars, so what could we do? Well, we solicited corporate sponsors back in the States for the sole purpose of returning to build a baseball field in the jungles of Bongo. Getting all the necessary equipment on site to complete this mission was no small task, I can assure you. Most of the roads surrounding this village were dirt or some form of gravel, so getting heavy equipment to the field location was the first major hurdle—or so we thought. When organizing trips like this, you are always looking for a way to trim costs to make the trip as affordable as possible. So in doing this, I mapped out an alternative route to Bongo through Costa Rica, which would require us to rent a car and drive from San Jose. Well, there was one problem with this great idea: unbeknownst to me, rental cars are not allowed across the border. So upon receiving this wonderful news standing at the rental car counter, there was only one option: hurry to the airport and pray there was a flight to David. Mind you, this flight only exists three days a week, but as usual, God was looking out for us and there was a flight leaving in an hour. Lost in all this was the fact that this extra flight was not in our budget and it was going to cost us over a $1,000 we did not have. So just like any other red-blooded American would do, I charged it! Like so many other times in my life, I trusted God's path, and of course, as you will see later in this chapter, he did not let us down.

Upon finally arriving in Bongo, we knew it was essential to clear and level this land before anything else could be done. Remember, we were at the base of a volcano, so to tell you there were a lot of rocks is an understatement. Some of these rocks were over four hundred pounds, so moving them by hand was not an option. We had also arranged, with the help of Turface Athletics, for a container to be delivered with field maintenance products, rakes, bases, a home plate, a mound, etc.

As I mentioned earlier, if you get too frustrated when things do not arrive in a timely fashion, you will walk around mad all the time. So while we waited for the equipment and container to show up, we started constructing a backstop out of bamboo. To my knowledge, it had never been done before, so we certainly didn't have a manual or prior experience to pull from. So we laid out the sixty-by-twenty-foot net we had dragged through customs in what looked like a body bag. You should have seen some of the looks we got in the airports, and it was certainly a topic for discussion with several armed agents until they opened it. Even then, it was hard to explain what we were doing with it and where we were taking it. We cut the biggest bamboo we could find and dug holes for support. Then we painted all the poles black and hung the net (it took three tries, but it was finally up and functional). Because of the tropical environment and rainy season approaching, we felt it was necessary to develop a drainage system around the field, so we used a pick ax to hand-dig a trench around the perimeter, and then we filled it with rocks. We even cut bamboo to make foul poles and painted them yellow. After two days of this, the heavy equipment showed up, and we started moving some dirt. It was the darkest soil I had ever seen in my life. It certainly made sense after seeing this why almost every inch of land in this village had some sort of crops on it.

We leveled and picked up rocks for three days with the help of local villagers. We ran our strings and installed bases and a pitching rubber. Game on! When I tell you the people of Bongo came out to see their new field, I mean it. It was lined from one end of the field to the other. On the day before our departure, we played all day long. First, the kids played, then the women played, and then the men played. Basically, people were coming out of the jungle from all directions to see what this was all about. Unfortunately, like all trips, our time was up in this wonderful place, but our team had one more stop before returning to the States. Remember Frank Melgar from our first trip to Panama?

I called him Panama Jack. We were headed to see his place and take him up on his offer.

All we knew was the name of his resort, Pacific Bay Resort, and a general direction to go in from Bongo toward the coast. You have to understand, there was no interstate system or reliable map to use. I remember on our first trip to Panama, Secundino got lost getting us to Bongo after detouring around the protest, and he lived there. However, through e-mail communication with Frank, I did have confidence we would get to the coast in close enough proximity to find it eventually. That uncertainty can be scary or very exciting depending on a person's perspective. Most of our lives are filled with certainty and not enough uncertainty. Uncertainty can cripple some and inspire others. It's all about your goals in life and what you strive to obtain from it. For me, I love surprises and going anywhere I have never been before. If I have never been there, there is a great chance I will experience and feel something I never have before. So many possible life-changing moments are missed every day because people are gripped with the fear of uncertainty.

After about a three-hour drive, we finally had no more land to drive on. We parked at a church and started asking around, and the answers we got shocked us, to say the least. Everyone we asked had the same answer: "You need a boat!" So we started asking local fishermen if they could take us, and finally one agreed to the price we were able to pay. It's hard to describe the feeling of heading out into the Pacific Ocean, unsure of where you will end up, trusting in someone you've never met before and what lies around the next corner. So for about forty-five minutes, we took in breathtaking views of the sun setting over what seemed like hundreds of islands just off the coast. Then the boat began to slow, and the fisherman began to point. We saw a set of stairs heading up the steep face of this island. As we got closer, two men appeared and began walking toward the shore. It felt like we were on an episode of *Fantasy Island,* except we were arriving in a boat and not "de plane." There was no dock, so when the boat came to a halt, we had to take our shoes off and carry our luggage out over the water. I guess Frank forgot to mention that he owned an island.

The two guys waiting on the beach took us to the top of the island and showed us our rooms. We did immediately notice that there was no air-conditioning and no television sets. It was not exactly what most people from the States would call a resort, but we soon figured out why it was precisely that. Frank had placed twelve of these rooms throughout the island, totally secluded from one another. There was a beautiful cove for kayaking and snorkeling on one side of the island. It even had hammocks nestled in the palm trees for a quick siesta. The other side of the island had a nice beach with a clear view of the ocean. The most impressive feature was the common eating area on the highest point of the island. Our dinner that first night was amazing, and the view was literally inspiring. We talked about the trip and how blessed we were to be in this exact place at this exact time. What if we had allowed our uncertainty to rule our decision in making this journey? It would have been much easier to stay another day in Bongo, where we felt comfortable, and then get on a plane and go back to our everyday lives. We would have missed a rare opportunity to look at the world through a different pair of glasses.

By the time we headed back to our rooms, it was dark. When I mean dark, you couldn't see your hand in front of your face.

As I described before, there were no modern amenities, so you lie in bed and just listen to the jungle. It's actually a great time to reflect on your life and think about your family. I would think about the legacy that I strive to leave behind when I am gone. The next day, we got up early to go explore the island. We saw howler monkeys, huge iguanas, and gorgeous birds. As we trekked around the outside of the island, we found caves to hike through that had passageways coming out the other side, farther down the shoreline. Not until several hours later would we figure out why those holes existed. Like most of the islands in the region, they were shaped by volcanic activity, so most of the formations were made of jagged black rock. After about three hours of hiking, we figured it was time to head back so as not miss a nicely prepared meal from the Pacific Bay Resort staff. Well, we waited just a little too long to head back because the tide had already started coming in. Those caves I spoke of earlier, they were completely filled with water. There were some dicey moments, but thank the good Lord we made it back and learned another very valuable lesson when it comes to Mother Nature.

At lunch, Frank got on to us about leaving too many lights on the night before because everything on the island runs on solar power. When he was finished giving us a hard time, he asked if we wanted to go fishing; of course we immediately said yes. None of us had ever been fishing in the Pacific Ocean, and I am pretty sure we all visualized it going down a bit different than it did. He told us to wait at the bottom of the stairs and his guy would come pick us up. I remember our conversation while we were waiting, and all of it had to do with where Frank kept his fishing boat. We had scoured the island quite a bit and didn't remember seeing one, so we figured maybe he called a friend of his to take us or it was hidden away in the interior of the island on one of the rivers. We were wrong on both accounts!

Slowly coming around the corner, we saw a glorified canoe with a motor on it. On the back, sitting cross-legged was, Jose, one of Frank's staff. As we were waiting for the boat to stop, I thought to myself, *Surely we aren't going fishing on the Pacific Ocean in this.* After a brief moment of anxiety while boarding, I sat down very cautiously and thought to myself again, *God didn't bring us this far to throw us in the ocean and be eaten by sharks, so let's roll with this and see how it goes.* Well, I can tell you this: we felt like a gnat on an elephant's butt. It seemed like the ocean would just swallow us at any moment, but after a short period of time, it was clear Jose knew what he was doing. As they say, this wasn't his first rodeo. There were definitely some anxious moments when a fifteen-foot swell was headed toward us or when we spotted a huge volcanic rock formation piercing through the water that we felt was surely unavoidable, but after a while, it was more relaxing than riding on a cruise ship. So we fished for a few hours until twilight and hauled in a few yellowtails that would end up on our dinner plates in the very near future. These are the types of experiences that shape our perspective on the world, and they are so different every place you visit. As Sydney J. Harris puts it, "Regret for things we did can be tempered by time; it is the regret for things we did not do that is inconsolable."

After another night of jungle music and deep thoughts, we were headed home. Often on your way back from a trip of this magnitude, your mind races. *What could we have done differently? What happened at home while I was gone? How long will it take for me to catch up? Will I take what I learned on this trip and apply it to my life? Can I inspire others to do more? Where will God's path take us next?* Well, as I pulled into my driveway and went to the mailbox, inside I found a check for almost the exact amount that we went over budget because of the unexpected flight we had to take. For me, as I stood alone in front of my house staring at this check in disbelief, with a tear in my eye, all I could think about was how I should have never doubted for a second that God would provide. He has shown us grace at every turn, and no circumstance we face will ever change that.

On our most recent trip to Panama, it truly felt like we had never left. Every time I return to Bongo, I get a sense of peace. My mind slows down, and a greater appreciation for all the things we take for granted on a daily basis is thrown right in my face. It is a very intimate experience for the guys who go. It gets dark early because of how close it is to the equator, so when we are done for the day, we have a lot of time to reflect on our experiences that day and invest in one another. When you are in the jungle, there is no rat race, no cell phone—just life!

Our goal for this trip was to establish a presence in Sortova that would be sustainable for years to come. All of the baseball equipment and Turface products we donated on previous trips had been moved to this community. After visiting the first day, there was renewed hope for what could be done, but it required building relationships with the local representative, school principal, and the physical education teacher. This started with a game of softball on Sunday afternoon that included the adult males from the community. Next, it was P.E. at the school, and that progressed to baseball clinics by the end of the week. We gave the kids hats, socks, and shirts, and donated equipment to the school so that training could continue after our departure. One evening, we went to Concepcion to speak with a local soccer club about our experiences and how sports can be such a driving force in an effort to serve others regardless of their circumstances. We also took two afternoons to redo the ceiling of a local church in Bongo, called Iglesia Evangelica Metodista. Of course, a trip to Bongo would not be complete without a few relaxing trips to the river. By the end of the trip, we were invited to a dinner hosted by the local representative that the governor even attended, and we secured spots for interns the following summer.

I think sometimes not knowing what's coming is better, especially when it comes to Volcan Baru Part 2. I tackled this beast when I was four years younger, and it was the hardest thing I had ever done physically. So to say I was a little apprehensive would be an understatement. As a leader, however, that can't show on your face or in your body language. On top of that, I had the great idea for us to spend the night on top, so we had twice as much gear and supplies. Wouldn't you know, by the time we reached the final two kilometers, it was raining sideways and freezing cold! So what do you do, give up or push on? Of course, you push on, just like in life! By the time everyone reached the top, we knew our plans for pitching tents and starting a fire were out the window. There would be no singing "Kumbayah" around the campfire. Fortunately for us, there is a police station on top of the mountain, so we ended up sleeping on the floor in a storage room. Wet, cold, and huddled together, our goal was just to make it through the night by tending to the guys who were suffering from altitude sickness and figuring out how to use the bathroom without indoor plumbing during a freezing cold rain storm and forty-mile-per-hour winds. It was interesting, to say the least, and no doubt an unforgettable experience for everyone.

We finished this trip on the Pacific Ocean. Of course, in

typical fashion, we headed toward a destination unknown but with some sort of general knowledge about the area. We did know if we kept driving, we would eventually hit the ocean. When we finally pulled into this little gravel parking lot and opened the van doors, you could hear the unmistakable sounds of waves crashing against the sand. There was a little outdoor restaurant with a covered tin roof and plastic tables and chairs. As we all walked through the sand of this deserted beach, we turned around, and there was Volcan Baru as the backdrop. It is hard to explain the range of emotions you feel when you see it. You have the euphoria of eight-foot Pacific Coast waves and the beautiful Costa Rican mountains off in the distance, but yet that replay over and over in your mind of a brutally exhausting climb to the top of that mountain. It was actually a perfect combination of all you are and all you strive to be. Of course, after pulling some tables together and sitting down to relax, a storm swept in off the coast and we were right in the middle of a lightning storm. It was like being at a Fourth of July fireworks show. Being from the south, I am not usually too keen on storms because a lot of times that means tornadoes, but for some reason, it was very tranquil. As I looked around at the guys hanging out with each other, thinking about the entire week, coupled with all these breathtaking features, all I could say to myself was, *This is perfect!*

CHAPTER 5

Africa

On beknownst to us, our work in Panama had not just helped change the culture of a small farming village but evidently was being noticed halfway around the world. The Youth Council of Limbe, Cameroon, saw pictures and read our story on Facebook. That's all the evidence I need to show me that social media has truly changed the way we live. So over the course of several months, I communicated with them via e-mail and planned our next trip to introduce the game of baseball to over three hundred kids who had never seen a bat, ball, or a glove before. During this time, I did the best I could to come up with a comprehensive itinerary with limited communication and a lot of faith. When I introduced the idea to our community, to say they were a little apprehensive would be an understatement.

There weren't too many mommies lining up to send their sons halfway around the world to a continent that had just experienced an ebola outbreak and was only a few countries away from where we were going. I even had to show my daughters how far apart the two countries were to reassure them there was no danger. Now just because there was no danger from a deadly disease doesn't mean it was the safest place in the world either. In the hour and a half it took from the airport in Douala to Limbe, we took a short cut to avoid bandits and were stopped twice by machine-gun-carrying guards. They were supposed to be checkpoints, but all it was, was a shakedown!

They asked for all of our passports, and that's when our driver, Dominque, went to arguing with these people. He knew what they wanted, and he wasn't having any of it. It was a very tense scene, watching someone we just met fight so passionately for us, and I would like to mention again these guys were armed. All we could hear him say while his arms were moving and pointing in the air was that these men were here to help our children and no one should be trying to take anything from them. We often discussed what we thought might have happened had he not been with us. At no point during our trip was he going to allow anyone to take advantage of us. Dominique was a godsend from the beginning until he dropped us off at the airport.

Now unfortunately not everyone was as honorable, and it took us almost two days to figure out who was really there in an effort to further our cause and who was trying to execute their own agenda. The latter was definitely more common. In the United States, we are so naive about the desperation people face on a daily basis and the hopelessness they feel. We came to find out, people were trying to use our organization and the work we were doing to elevate their status in the community in hopes of acquiring visas for their families.

At the end of the day, none of these obstacles changed our mission; it just made it a little more difficult. We started by doing an interview at the local Christian radio station in hopes of creating interest in a sport that had never been played before.

Would kids and their parents even show up? Yes, I had been told by leaders in the community they would come, but you truly never know until you show up, and in this case, even after you show up. Our first location was beside a cornfield on the outskirts of town, in close proximity to what they would consider a neighborhood. We showed up, and there were three kids kicking a soccer ball.

My heart dropped! "Well, boys, we didn't come here to sit in the van." We got out and starting throwing the baseball around, and I kid you not, in twenty minutes there were over one hundred kids in that field. It seemed like they were coming from everywhere. It felt like I was in that scene from *Field of Dreams* when players from the past started coming out of the cornfield to play ball. The most famous line of that movie, "If you build it, they will come," kept replaying over and over in my head as this was happening. After my amazement wore off, we had to figure what to do with over one hundred kids who had never swung a bat or thrown a ball. The kids put gloves on both hands, used the wrong end of the bat, and certainly had no idea how to throw a ball.

My main concern was safety and the kids having a good time. Luckily for us, we had a lot of whiffle balls. Our photographer had a drone, so that was a huge source of entertainment, watching kids chase it around in total amazement. They were just as amazed to see their picture on a camera, as was evident by the swarms of children surrounding the cameraman when he allowed even a glimpse into what he was taking pictures of. Despite not knowing anything about the sport of baseball, the kids had a blast, and several of them picked it up very quickly. It never ceases to amaze me, regardless of the country, demographics, or economic circumstances—kids are just kids! They all have smiles on their faces and completely appreciate any amount of time you are willing to share with them.

This pattern continued for several days in multiple locations throughout the community. In some places, the kids were older, and the facilities may have been a little different, but in each place, one constant remained: a desire to experience something new despite what circumstances they may be facing as soon as they left those fields. Some of the young men we worked with were so gifted athletically and were so easy to work with. If they lived in the United States, they would be preparing to play major college athletics; instead, they would leave those fields and prepare the next day for the fishing boat or the coffee fields. It's an eye-opening experience for people on these trips to finally realize just how fortunate they are to have every opportunity in the world to succeed. Until they see this firsthand, they have no idea that in places all over the globe, that's just not the case.

When developing any itinerary for these trips, of course, you have to be prepared for the fact that some things just are not going to work out. For this trip, my contact told me there were American soldiers working with the Cameroonians at their naval base in Limbe. So, of course, I thought it would be a great idea to visit them and let them know how much we appreciated their service and even invite them to join us when working with the kids. So as we approached the main gate with anticipation at our scheduled time and were met by soldiers carrying automatic weapons claiming they had no idea what we were talking about, it didn't shock me in the least.

Dominique proceeded to haggle with one of the guards, which was definitely a common occurrence when we tried to do anything for anyone or with anyone on a daily basis. After they spoke, we were told to wait off to the side in a small field while this soldier asked around. After about twenty minutes, a gold-armor-plated Toyota Hilux drove through the gate and approached us. The two guys in the truck just sat there sizing us up. Not knowing what to do, I got out and went to talk to them. You could tell as I started speaking, they were on edge, checking their 360 constantly. So I started telling them our story about what we were doing in Cameroon and that we just wanted to spend time with them if possible. The guy in the driver's seat, I later found out, was the commanding officer (Chili is what they called him). He looked at me and said, "No one knows we are here."

After he said that, I knew these guys were an elite group there for a specific reason, so the edginess made sense. The more we talked, however, you could tell he felt more at ease, and they actually invited us back to their hooch. After introducing us to his team, we just sat down and hung out. We told them about our plans for the week and asked them if they would like to be a part of it, but anytime we asked a question about anything relating to their group, every soldier immediately looked at Chili as to say, "Can we answer that?" It was a unique experience to see that dynamic unfold in front of us. These guys were the best of the best, and you could tell it. They were all ripped, muscles everywhere, and the most humble guys on the planet. It truly made me proud to be in the same room with them and come to find out a few of them played college baseball.

So during the week, they came and helped with clinics. We took them out to dinner one night, and we even played beach volleyball with them. I felt like we were in the movie *Top Gun*. At the end of the trip, the night before we left, we went back to the base and gave them baseball equipment so they could play with the Cameroonian soldiers they were training. They presented us with patches and decals, and not only that, they proceeded to tell us how much of an amazing week it was and how much they appreciated being a part of it. I can remember listening to these words and thinking to myself, *I can't even reveal this guy's name because his family doesn't even know where he is, and he is thanking us.* This was not one of the highlights you see on CNN. We were standing in the midst of the sacrifice these guys make on a daily basis for our freedom. It was such a privilege and an honor to be around them for just the briefest of moments, but it also confirmed for me how the smallest act of service to others can impact lives in the most unlikely of places. I will never forget the time we spent with those young men, and I am quite sure they will never know the lasting impression they left on me.

Another very eye-opening experience for us was visiting the Slave Trade Port of Bimbia. This was one of the major slave ports on the West African coast for over two hundred years. According to locals, not much had been documented here until recently because it had remained hidden under thick tropical rainforest, but mainly because villagers of Bimbia believe the area is cursed; as they explained it to us, "No one who went there ever came back!" Regardless of how uncomfortable it was, I felt it was extremely important for our team to learn about this awful time in history and invest our hearts and minds in this beautiful country.

I am not going lie: it was kind of eerie walking this long path lined with huge bamboo pods; lush, green trees; flowers, and the sound of waves crashing in the foreground, knowing what may lie ahead. As we drew closer to our destination, the hairs began to stand up on the back of my neck, and all I can say is I felt a strong presence as we began to look upon these ruins that were being taken back by the jungle. I couldn't take my eyes off of these stone troughs that slaves would have to eat out of while being chained and shackled. Believe it or not, that wasn't the hardest pill for me to swallow: it was the *door of no return!* There was a small river that ran up into the jungle from the ocean, and built on its bank was the last place these slaves would ever see of their homeland. Basically, it only consisted of stone pillars equipped with the chains of bondage and two doors: one to come in, and the other facing the river, which these young men and women would walk through and never be seen again.

Recent historical findings have documented nearly two hundred slave ship voyages that left Cameroon bound mostly for plantations in the Americas. These ships would anchor on Nicholls Island just off the coast and send small boats up the river. As we were listening to this very vivid depiction of events, you could see mouths drop, eyes get big, and even streams of tears. It is really hard to explain the emotions you go through if you have never been to such a historically significant—and at the same time unbelievably horrific—place. It is quite certainly one of—if not the most—powerful places I have ever been.

CHAPTER 6

Colombia

One of our more recent trips was to the interior of Colombia. Contrary to popular belief, baseball is not given much thought there on a daily basis. When talking to people back in the States about the upcoming trip, they assumed all Latin American countries love baseball, but the truth is, soccer is still king! Our team for this trip was by far the biggest group to date: twenty-six servants, ranging from ages sixteen to fifty-two. Our team represented several local high schools, colleges, and leaders from the community. I truly believe it's a testament to not only our prior work to date but God's path for More Than A Game and all of its volunteers.

One of our goals for this trip was to introduce baseball to children in Puente Iglesias, a small village at the base of the Andes Mountains. We would also give them baseball equipment, uniforms, Bibles, and hopefully some sort of structure to continue training after our departure. We would spend five days in the country at a beautiful farmhouse, locally known as a Finca, so graciously provided by Patrick Powers. It was located about halfway up one of the mountain passes overlooking the river. The views were breathtaking and really left us in awe as we watched the sun come up or clouds roll in below us. I don't think any of us had ever stayed above the clouds before. The boys would get up at six every morning and pick fresh fruit and get eggs from the hen houses. We also had a list of chores for them to complete around the farm during our time there. Patrick is a businessman from Texas, originally from Chicago, who spends a good deal of time in Colombia. He felt our organization could not only help the kids of this region learn about baseball but also open doors for them that could change the course of their lives forever.

Six months prior, he helped obtain visas for two young men, Jose Mercado and Mateo Porras, in hopes of them returning with us to pursue their dreams of getting an American education and playing baseball in college. After just a few days with these two wonderful young men, several guys had already offered to open their homes to Jose and Mateo upon our return to the States. Before we started clinics on a Monday, we took a horseback ride through the mountains to the city of Jericho at about nine thousand feet above sea level. Not many of us had much experience with horses, and there were a few tense moments when the trails narrowed and you could see rocky gorges several thousand feet below. All that seemed to fade away as we came around this one turn and the awe-inspiring Andes Mountains were in full view for everyone to see. It's really hard to describe the beauty. To me, it feels like you are looking at a painting; even though you know it's real, it still looks fake. Near the top, we stopped for lunch, which consisted of rice, pork, and plantains wrapped in a banana leaf. While we were eating, one of the horses got spooked and started a chain reaction that pulled most of the rickety barbed wire fence out of the ground and scared us all half to death.

After lunch, we made our way to the top of the mountain and took a short break to visit with a farmer and see the process of harvesting coffee beans. During this stop, he invited us to have fresh bananas with him and just hang out for a while. If you have never had fruit freshly picked, I highly recommend it. It will blow your mind how much different it tastes from buying it from a store in the States. It hasn't been processed, preserved, and shipped yet, so not only is it sweeter, it even smells and looks different. I had experienced this before in Africa when getting a pineapple on the side of the road, as well as picking oranges off the trees in Panama and even the first morning in Colombia when we had freshly picked mangos with breakfast. We tend to think everything is better in America, but that goes back to getting out of your comfort zone and experiencing new cultures. There are so many things in this world about which we are completely ignorant. We just accept what we know to be true because that's the path of least resistance!

Shortly after this, we all loaded up on a really cool bus that took us to Jericho. This bus had open sides, wooden bench seating, and was painted every color of the rainbow. They dropped us off in the town square at one of the most beautiful churches I had ever seen. After walking through the church, we split up into groups, nosed around in several small stores, and checked out the open-air market on the plaza.

The next day, we climbed a volcano, Sierro Bravo (10,800 feet). One noticeable difference from the volcano in Panama was that it was covered by the jungle canopy for just about the entire hike. This made the humidity much worse. This hike was also straight up the face, so we definitely had to do more climbing. That being said, there weren't the long stretches of vertical walking like in Panama, so it only took us about three and a half hours. When one of my dear friends of over twenty years, Mike Getkin, made it to the top, he dropped like a sack of potatoes and curled up in the fetal position. Not bad for someone in his mid-fifties, though! When he finally got up, all I could do was hug him and tell him how proud I was of him. I will never forget sharing that experience with him. We had lunch, took pictures, got some video footage, and soaked in the moment before heading back down.

When I took a moment to look around, I could genuinely see the sense of accomplishment on everyone's faces. It is always amazing to watch the guys interact with each other while pushing themselves physically and mentally. You can learn so much about people when they are put in extreme circumstances. Are you going to give up in life when it gets hard or are you going to push through it and become a better person for having persevered during the tough times? That's really what it's all about, and they all passed with flying colors. Believe me when I tell you, that hike was no joke!

The next morning, we headed to the village of Puente Iglesias to do a baseball clinic for all the kids in the school there. Because of construction on the bridge, we had to carry all the equipment we planned on donating about three-quarters of a mile to the field. When we finally arrived at the field we were going to use, there was a man there weed-eating grass that was waist high. As I told you earlier, not many things go according to plan on these trips. Expect the unexpected and just roll with it. We split into four large groups and taught the kids throwing, fielding, hitting, and base running. There were even three of the local policia who stopped by and participated. After we were finished, we presented the principal of the school with ten bags of equipment, dental supplies, and one hundred Bibles.

The second half of our trip would take place around the city of Medellin. With almost 3 million people, different challenges would lay ahead, with the biggest being transportation. Despite this, we arranged to do clinics and equipment donations in Evingado and Santa Margarita. We also met with the mayor's sports organization, Inder, in hopes of promoting baseball in the city. In the end, it was about the kids we spent time with and how they blessed us every day.

One day at a clinic in Evingado, several of the moms went home and made empanadas for everyone, just to show their appreciation. In Santa Margarita, one of the kids went to his house during the clinic to get us water to show his appreciation for our presence there. It's hard to explain the feeling you have inside when something like that happens because you can see all around you the circumstances in which the kids live (no running water, etc.)—and their first thought is to provide for you. It is extremely humbling, to say the least!

After doing clinics during the day, it had been arranged for us to play the Medellin Select Team in a three-game series at the Stadio Medellin Villeges. We didn't put together a roster to play real games for this trip, but we made the most of it, and the kids had a blast. We made flyers and had the boys pass them out during the day to promote the events. When the lights came on, the little kids showed up! Our kids were signing autographs before the games just like they were in the big leagues! They never stopped smiling from start to finish. One of the local kids passed his phone to the dugout, and the message read, "You are our idols!" That had a big impact on the boys; how we take for granted something as a simple as playing a baseball game.

CHAPTER 7

Dominican Republic

Our most recent trip was to the Dominican Republic. With the help of Pittsburgh Pirates' Latin American Pitching Coordinator, Amaury Telemaco, as well as support from the Pirates' Charities Foundation, the Pirates' Academy, and Turface Athletics, we achieved so much in such a short period of time. In just six days, we were able to build a field in La Romana, renovate a field in Boca Chica, administer two clinics, visit an orphanage, go to a Toros baseball game, go dune-buggy riding, swim in a cave, and visit the beach. We even managed to squeeze in Thanksgiving dinner on foreign soil. We also introduced the first women of MTAG. Never before had we opened up one our trips to females, and the fact that three of them were my wife and two daughters made it extremely special to me.

Our team consisted of fifteen in all, ranging in ages from twelve to sixty, and hailing from Alabama, California, and Georgia. We had current high school players, former college and professional players, as well as community leaders who had never played before. It was a great group with a lot to offer these two different communities. We had only decided a month before that we were going to make this trip happen, which is a much shorter timeframe than normal. I had been introduced to Kyle Stark, assistant general manager of the Pirates, during the spring by a mutual friend, Anthony Randall. I met Anthony, a ranger and chaplain for the US Army, through a free clinic we did that winter in Columbus, Georgia. We hit it off immediately, and he wanted to help us any way he could, which started with his contacts in the Pirates' organization. After visiting with Kyle during spring training, he agreed to help in any way possible. He started by making sure we had a significant donation of equipment for our trip to Colombia and put me in contact with their key personnel in the Dominican Republic and the director of Pirates' charities.

My first e-mail was met with open arms and excitement at the prospect of us coming to the Dominican Republic. In preparing for this trip, I was already significantly impacted by developing a great friendship with Amaury. I knew right away, after our first time on the phone, that we had the same passion for serving others as well as the same appreciation of all that God had blessed us with! So, it didn't shock me when he met us at the airport despite his busy schedule with the Pirates and that he made sure we were comfortable in our new surroundings before he left for the night.

Our team stayed at the Good Samaritan House, which consisted of dorm-style accommodations, a common area for meals, and a thirty-year-old school bus to take us anywhere we needed to go. An added bonus: the best dessert I have ever tasted each night after dinner from a little local bakery. No matter his schedule, our friend seemed to show up for that part of the evening (we called it dessert with Amaury)! Our first day started outside the Toro's stadium with a clinic and field building. When we arrived, the coach, Varon William, and his kids were waiting on us. Before we could start, he finished having church service with them. As we begin setting up to administer the clinic, it was a good opportunity to evaluate the piece of land available for a field. Basically, it was a forgotten piece of land tucked next to a water tower and beside a ten-foot-high wall, protecting it from the highway. Not to mention it was covered with boulders and trash, and overburden. So what looked impossible to start became our mission for three days.

We immediately recognized that the only way it would happen would be to rent heavy equipment and really get the coach and his players to buy into the project. Well, that certainly happened and then some. We even made a backstop out of huge rocks and painted the More Than A Game logo on it. On Tuesday after we finished work for the day, we headed to the Ninos De Cristo orphanage to donate school supplies and children's books. The director was so appreciative, and we felt likewise for just having the opportunity to share time with those amazing kids. Before leaving La Romana's newest field Wednesday afternoon, we played games with the kids and donated equipment, uniforms, and Bibles. The coach and heavy equipment operators even got some cuts in.

That night, we headed to a Toro's game to experience a Winter Ball game in the Dominican. It was nonstop excitement from start to finish, regardless of what was happening on the field. There was a pep section with drums and chants, and when they weren't cheering, which wasn't very often, loud music was blaring throughout the stadium. It was so much different from a game in the States; you could feel the passion they had for their team and the game of baseball. We saw a relief pitcher throw a pitch one hundred miles per hour, and the mascot body-slammed a stuffed dummy behind home plate! We had an amazing time.

We scheduled Thursday as a day of rest and planned an excursion for everyone. It started with dune-buggy driving through coffee plantations and fresh-water swimming in caves, and finished with a visit to the beach. No one on the team had ever done any of those things before, so it was a special day for all involved. That apprehensive look on people's faces before jumping into a cave is priceless, and then when they hit the water and the temperature takes their breath away, it's even better. Facing that uncertainty in any aspect of life is what builds character and confidence so that we can face challenges in life head-on. We finished that night with a special Thanksgiving dinner we had arranged away from the dorm.

After we returned, Amaury invited my family and me over to his house to hang out with him and his wife. We had a wonderful time just talking about what was going on in our lives, the trip up to that point, and pretty much life in general. When people are genuine, most of the time, they want to talk about you and not themselves. You would have never known he played in the big leagues for nine years because it was like sitting out behind my house, watching college football with the guys on a Saturday afternoon. There were no hidden agendas, just sincerity. Oh and his wife asked the girls if they wanted to take a hot shower, and of course they couldn't get upstairs fast enough!

We headed out early the next day to Boca Chica to renovate a field near the Pirates' Academy. Unlike our first project, this field had a good framework and just needed a facelift. We started by edging and removing all the weeds from the entire infield. Then we built a mound, rebuilt the home plate area, and added conditioner to the infield. The Pirates' Academy sent guys to do a clinic with the kids. They also helped us pass out all the equipment and uniforms, and informed us they planned on adding a fence to the outfield after our departure as well as committing field maintenance help on a monthly basis. We finished up by speaking with all the players and presenting them with Bibles. That evening, we headed to a spot Amaury recommended at a nearby beach to have dinner and have our MTAG Emmy Awards (a tradition we started in Colombia). Each person gets an award and gives a brief speech about their experience for the week and what the trip has meant to them personally. It is a great time of personal growth and fellowship.

The final morning, we were up early, out of the dorm, and headed to the orphanage one last time. We wanted to donate some shoes and clothes before we headed out. Next, we arranged to meet Coach William at the field in La Romana to give him Turface Moundmaster Blocks so he could build a pitching mound and home plate for the kids after we left. We also brought more equipment and clothing to be dispersed at a later date. He was so appreciative and prayed for us. It was a truly special moment! We had arranged to tour the Pirates Baseball Academy and have lunch before our flight left, so that was our next stop. You could tell during the tour that building servant-leadership qualities in their players is a high priority. Quotes from Roberto Clemente, the namesake for the highest Community Service Award in the major leagues, adorned the walls. Operations Assistant Emmanual Gomez, who gave us the tour, was very quick to talk about helping others in need and developing the man ahead of the player. It was quite impressive because I could tell it had been ingrained in him from the top of the organization. We had a great lunch in the cafeteria and probably would have eaten more but were running short on time.

We arrived at the airport with just enough time to say our good-byes. One group was headed to Atlanta and the other to San Francisco. It's hard to describe how close you can get to someone in just a week under these circumstances, but I'm pretty sure it's because of the vulnerability you feel when taking on the unknown and pushing through whatever is thrown at you. It's very intense at times, and allows us to let our guard down and really get to know one another. That includes our bus driver (Colbert) and our translators (Gia and Luis) as well. There were hugs, tears of joy, and promises to stay in touch. One thing was for certain: none of us would ever forget these people or this experience.

These trips are so important, not only for the service we may give but the deep-seated roots we return with. Each culture we experience is different in so many ways, yet the one thing we always leave with is a greater appreciation for and perspective on life. It is such a powerful force in determining how you choose to attack the rest of your life as a student, a professional, and even as a parent.

"Nothing is more disgraceful than that an old man should have nothing to prove that he has lived long, except his years." -Seneca

CHAPTER 8

Building a Program

As I get older, I certainly gain a greater appreciation for my former players and teams. We have been blessed over the years with so many great victories and, equally as important, with our share of losses. That's right: recognizing that some losses are as—if not more—important than victories is a key ingredient to becoming a successful coach and leader in any profession. "If you want twice the success, double your rate of failure," said Jeff Olson in *The Slight Edge*. Having great mentors allowed me to develop a coaching philosophy over four years as an assistant that put many factors ahead of just winning. Winning is a byproduct of so many little things that coaches lose sight of when allowing the pressure of winning to affect their decision-making. I always quote Cal Ripken Sr. to my players: "If we do all the little things right, then we'll never have a big thing to worry about."

When I took over as head baseball coach, there were ten items that I identified over the course of those four years as an assistant coach that would be the building blocks for my coaching philosophy.

1. Decision-Making: Faith, Family, Education, Baseball
2. Rules & Regulations
3. Daily Responsibilities
4. Facility Upgrades (five-year plan)
5. Commitment to Community Service
6. College Recruiting
7. Team Camp
8. Scheduling
9. Branding
10. Alumni

I would like to examine them with you and how they directly tie into ultimately achieving our goals.

Rules and Regulations: Accountability is so crucial in establishing leadership. I am convinced that young men in our society desperately need a blueprint that will help them mature and realize there are consequences for their actions. Our rules and regulations are not extreme by any means. They are expected to be on time, dressed and groomed properly, maintain academic standards, and treat people with respect on and off the field. Equally as important, they should never draw attention to themselves over the program, which includes profanity, questioning an umpire, or throwing a piece of equipment. As athletes, they are role models in our community and should act accordingly. All these things will be expected of them in the professional world, so why not now?

Daily Responsibilities: Every player has multiple assignments on a daily basis. Much like real life, there is a checklist. If it's not done, there are consequences. This could be anything from practice equipment and facility cleanliness to field upkeep and game-day procedures. It's really gratifying to see players pass down their knowledge to younger players from year to year and truly take pride in their responsibilities. Players will actually request certain tasks in advance for the next year. Make no mistake about it: kids want structure and leadership because they all strive to be successful.

Facility Upgrades: I think it is extremely important to stress improvement, no matter how great or small. I also feel sweat equity is a key ingredient to developing long-lasting pride in any program. For our program, I had a five-year plan and stuck to it. Whatever it took, whomever I had to beg, however many fundraisers it took, and however many hours of backbreaking work were required, we were going to do it together. We carried cinder blocks, shingles, trusses, siding, plywood, and beams, and laid sod by hand. There have been thousands of hours over the years from coaches, players, and parents dedicated to our vision. No matter how great our facility looks, we want to ingrain the mindset of never being satisfied. It may only be one small project a year, but it's progress nonetheless. If we are not going forward; we are going backward.

Community Service: There is no better way to create a culture of selflessness than serving others. Every year, as a team, we perform community service projects. We have worked at homeless shelters, battered women's shelters, child advocacy centers, disaster-relief aid programs, and one year we even got to work on an Extreme Makeover Home Edition. In addition, we host father/son and Little League instructional clinics.

College Recruiting: Probably one of the best and worst parts of my job is working to get our players to the next level. It's the best when you see kids realize their dreams and the worst when the harsh reality sets in that it is not going to happen. My approach has always been to knock on as many doors as necessary to help a young man with his goal of playing college baseball. The days of waiting for college coaches to find one of your players is long gone; it is essential that you are proactive. If any of my players are truly sincere, show me the passion that is required, and have the ability, then I refuse to give up. This requires late-night phone calls, recommendation letters, finding the right showcases, and being flexible enough to pile some players in your truck and take them to a tryout at a moment's notice. I have driven kids over eight hours to a camp that I thought was necessary. It is extremely important that you are always truthful with college coaches when recommending a player because you are building a reputation that will last forever. Every year, the relationships you develop with coaches will continually grow and increase the pool that you can call upon. Because of your honesty in the past, they trust you and will give your players a legitimate evaluation. Just in the last thirteen years, we have been blessed to send sixty-seven players to the next level. In 2005, we had nine kids sign from one team.

Team Camp: I believe anytime you have the opportunity as a coach to get your players away from home and out of their comfort zone, it is definitely a good thing. Team camp is perfect for that. They have to be up at a certain time; get to breakfast, lunch, and dinner on time; and adhere to dorm curfew. It's all about accountability. Mommy is not there to wake them up, wash their clothes, and buy them snacks. In addition, it's usually 95 degrees in the summer where we live, so they are tested mentally and physically by a full schedule of practicing and games. Depending on where you chose to take your guys, there should be ample opportunities for team-building exercises. We have been to many different colleges and universities, but for the last several years, we have gone to Berry College in the North Georgia Mountains. As a team, we hike to the top of the mountain, where all the upcoming seniors must address the team. These seniors give their expectations for next season and tell everyone what the Glenwood baseball program means to them. It is a chance for the younger guys to really see how important this whole process is and what they are a part of.

Scheduling: Each year, I have made every effort to put together the toughest schedule possible. Of course, some years are more difficult than others, but it is a definite priority. It's not only the teams you are playing but when you play them as well. I will purposely schedule a really good program after a big weekend tournament to test our mental toughness. On paper, the game will look unwinnable because the opposing team will have their number one pitcher rested and we will be throwing our number seven pitcher. We also play immediately after being off for spring break for five days. Did they have too much fun on their time off or did they show some sort of self-control? I have scheduled a doubleheader on the road after prom on several occasions. Will they put the team first by getting to bed at a decent hour or stay up all night with their friends? We've played several nationally ranked teams over the years, and it has only made us better regardless of the outcome on the scoreboard.

Branding: This is so crucial in the community when trying to build a program. The first step in this process was to create one unified logo. I know it sounds easy, but when you are talking about fourteen sports, the Booster Club, the PTO, and every academic club, it takes time to make that happen—not only managing it internally but working with vendors to make sure the correct logo is used every time. When I got here, I bet we used five different Gs and three different mascots. The goal is for anyone in our community—and for that matter, anyone in our state—to immediately identify the logo with the school when they see it. It's not only the logo—it's the gear the kids, parents, and alumni wear. The first two things I purchased after the logo change were license plates and window decals, and I got them put on as many cars as possible. Unfortunately, perception is a huge part of it. When little kids watch us play and we have good-looking uniforms and hats, it matters! When we have our camps, the team shop is stocked with what we wear on the field.

Alumni: I knew when taking over a program that had experienced so much success in the past, involving the alumni would be crucial. I immediately reached out to all the baseball alumni I knew personally and shared my five-year plan for facility improvements. I would also invite them to big games and, of course, an occasional alumni game. Nothing fires people up more than returning to their glory years, and it doesn't hurt to show off all the progress you've made with their contributions. It gives them ownership and a sense of pride because they know they have helped lay a foundation for many years to come. What is extremely awesome to see now, several years later, is that some of their children are beginning to make their way through the program and reap the rewards. Nothing pleases me more than when guys go off to college to play and they bring their teammates back with them for the weekend to show off our facilities.

CHAPTER 9

Magical Seasons

I can remember my first meeting with the team like it was yesterday; some things you just don't forget. As I approach twenty years in this profession and I begin to think back about truly special moments, some would be surprised that memories are not of holding up state championship trophies. Make no mistake about it: I am extremely proud of those on-field accomplishments because of how hard all the guys worked to achieve their goals and how unselfish each and every one of them had to be in serving something greater than themselves. It's the off-field memories that seem to spur more feelings of joy and accomplishment. I know eventually those victories will fade away, but it's the hundreds of great young men's lives I've been privileged to be a part of that matter the most: helping them mature from adolescence to become better fathers, husbands, and servants in this world. No one can convince me that our success over the years hasn't been a direct correlation to putting all these other criteria ahead of winning.

However, I would be remised in not sharing several truly special moments from years gone by—some highlights and even low lights that somewhat paint a small picture of our program during my tenure. When you take over a program as steeped in tradition as Glenwood, there are inherited expectations. They had not won a baseball state championship since 1993, the year Tim Hudson (four-time all-star, World Series Champion) graduated. Prior to that, the baseball program had won fourteen state championships in twenty-three years of existence. So it would seem like the pressure was on me to win a championship, but I never felt that way. I did have plenty of alumni tell me periodically, "You know, we haven't won a championship in a long time!" I was fine with it because I had confidence in what we were doing and how we were doing it. As you get older, you gain a greater appreciation of the process and not the results. The journey is so much more important, and it's never more evident than when you take some time to really reflect on how you got there.

When you have coached as long as I have, the sixty- to seventy-hour-per-week grind makes the years fly by and, to be honest, run together. There are, however, moments that seem forever burned into your memory. They tend to come in waves, and I can't explain what triggers them; some are good, and some bad. In our program, we have parents who have been around since I started coaching because I have coached as many as three of their sons. They do a good job of bringing up things from the past as well as former players telling stories when they get together. "Hey, coach, you remember the time when …?" The players tell these stories with such passion, and their faces light up like kids opening presents at Christmas. Trust me when I tell you, all these stories are not of game-winning home runs or striking out the final batter to win a state championship. Most of the time, they are stories of adversity, mistakes, and life-teaching moments.

Very few times have I ever heard them talking about individual accomplishments. Even though these things may seem trivial, they are a blessing and continually remind me of why I got into coaching in the first place.

I would like to share some of these memories, highs, and lows with everyone so that you may see through my eyes why I feel so blessed that God has allowed me to be a part of something so special. I think it is important to start at the beginning and tell these stories chronologically because so often people only focus on success and the number of championships, but in reality, your program, business, or even family is built on a series of actions or decisions made when you experience failure. I think when you really dig into your memories, you will find that the great times are often a result of or at least directly correlated to what you would classify as the bad times.

Infield Fly Rule: In my first year as head coach, we were playing in the Edgewood Tournament Championship early in the season against Macon-East Academy from Montgomery. We had a three-run lead going into the last inning and dropped three fly balls that never left the infield, with runners in scoring position. We lost the game. So what did we do on Monday? I turned the sound system on as loud as possible, and we hit fly balls to the infielders for hours. We hit them tennis balls so they were harder to catch and did sprints between rounds. I very rarely get mad about a physical mistake, which my players will attest to. You will never see me take someone out in the middle of an inning for making an error. Mental mistakes, on the other hand, are very hard for me to accept because it's something you can control. "Chance favors the prepared mind!" It's all about intense, controlled focus.

Ball off the Head: Also, in my first year as a head coach, having already won the first game in the state semifinals, we were leading Macon-East, 5–0. Kyle Tidwell had hit a grand slam in the first inning, and we were cruising. By the seventh inning, however, we only had a one-run lead with two outs, and they had runners at second and third. A routine ground ball was hit to our second baseman, Drew Edwards—who, by the way, had not committed an error all season. So, of course, what happens? A bad hop. The ball goes off his head, into right field. Both runs score, and we lose the game! You see these types of things happen in baseball all the time, and I think that's why I love the game so much. There are so many variables. Drew could not have done anything different. He did everything right, and we still lost; such is life. Wouldn't you know it, we lost the next game, and our season was over. In a matter of seconds, we went from sitting in the catbird's seat, rested and waiting for our opponent in the finals, to picking up the pieces of our shattered dreams. "So close, yet so far away."

The Homerun: I told you about the ground ball off the head in the state semifinals, but what I haven't told you is how we made it to the semifinals. We were down by two runs in the bottom of the seventh, with two runners on and two outs. In steps our senior catcher, William Gaston. He was leading the team in walks and hit by pitches by a considerable margin, so of course I thought for sure he would crowd the plate and get plunked. Nope; first pitch, he hits a walk-off three-run homerun to right centerfield. I still have the picture of him being mobbed at the plate hanging on my office wall. As a first-year head coach, I think you never grasp the gravity of a situation like that while it's happening or what it may mean to your program down the road because you're just caught up in the celebration. It's not until years later, when you glance up at the picture on the wall, you truly have a real appreciation for just having been present for that moment in these kid's lives.

Thirteen Errors: As I explained earlier about scheduling being a priority in the program, it's not just who you play but also where you play them. My second year as head coach, we played Tattnall Square at Columbus State University. It was one of the most embarrassing losses I have ever experienced as a coach. Not only did we make thirteen errors and get beat 13–2, we did it in front of a college coaching staff against a great program (Tattnall Square) from Macon, Georgia. And they were coached by one of my former teammates in college. I wanted to crawl under a rock and hide. As a young coach, it's hard to watch this unfold and not be angry because you think it is a direct reflection of your ability. You have stuck your neck out to get an awesome venue, promoted it in the community as two historic programs in neighboring states, and you see it as an opportunity to promote what the program is all about. Instead, your kids look unmotivated and have a complete lack of focus. Coaches always have a choice when these things happen, and trust me, when you coach for long enough, they will happen. So, feel sorry for yourself and come up with a long list of excuses or use it a building block and teachable moment to propel your team forward. So the next day, we took ground balls for hours. I made them take ground balls with no gloves. They did sprints between rounds, and they even did push-ups between rounds so their arms were tired. The point was not to punish them but to make them understand there was no excuse for a lack of focus, regardless of physical fatigue.

Breaking Curfew: Part of building a program is holding young men accountable for their actions. Putting rules and regulations in place is essential, but enforcing them is even more critical. In 2005, we took a trip to Mobile, Alabama, during spring break to play a nationally ranked team out of Louisiana and the top-ranked team in our association, Mobile Christian. We had played Central Private on Friday and got beat twice, and we were scheduled to play a doubleheader on Saturday. Curfew at the hotel that night was set for 11:00 p.m. Wouldn't you know, three starters were not in their room at bed check. Now these boys weren't out on the town or doing anything terrible; they were just not where they were supposed to be when they were supposed to be. One of the guys, Will Stillwell, was just sitting out in the hall, talking to his girlfriend. So I benched all three of them and told them that their attitudes as teammates that day would determine how long that would last. We got beat pretty bad in the first game, and we were losing the second game 4–3 going into the seventh. The boys I benched had sat there all day and cheered for their teammates without pouting, so I pinch-hit them consecutively. We scored two runs, won the game 5–4, and went on to win twenty-five consecutive games for Glenwood's first state championship in twelve years.

Throwing the Helmet: During my second year on our playoff run in the state semifinals, I had to sit our starting center fielder, Brett Worthington, when he threw his helmet in disgust after making an out. For me, it wasn't a tough decision because the precedent had been set and no matter what the circumstances are, the program comes first. It not being a hard decision in that moment doesn't make it an easy thing to deal with when the dust settles. When you look around and a four-year starter and two-hole hitter is sitting on the bench, it sets in. Not because you may lose because of it but because someone who has meant so much to the program is not out there with his teammates, trying to achieve a goal they have worked so hard for. If you look the other way because it's the semifinals, what message does that send your kids in the most important game of all: the game of life!

Dominant Pitching: I let the cat out of the bag about winning the 2005 State Championship, but what I remember is how dominant we were on the mound against a very good team from Faith Academy. They didn't get a runner past second base in both of our victories, and guess who was game 1 starter: Brett Worthington. The same guy I benched the week before was about to pitch the game of his life. Following him for game 2 was Chris Minney, and when we got to that point, the smart money was on us. You see, Chris was 44–4 for his career in high school and college. I liked our chances. He did not disappoint, throwing a complete game 3 hitter. What I also remember is how well we played defensively. Our shortstop, Eric Skinner, had as good a series as I've ever seen and was named MVP because of it. We didn't have power pitchers; we relied on pounding the strike zone, making plays, playing small ball, and grinding it out. What I like about those types of teams is they are usually disciplined, tough, and remain focused when the pressure is on. I think about this team with such pride and couldn't imagine a better group of young men to share my first state championship with.

Clubhouse Eviction: In 2007, we were about fifteen games into the season, and we were 8–7. This was very frustrating considering we returned all but one starter from a team that lost in the semifinals the year before. Not to mention we already had seven kids sign college scholarships and had what some would argue was as talented a starting nine as the program has ever had. I began noticing a lot of complacency and, to be honest, ungratefulness, so I kicked them out of our brand-new clubhouse. Picture twenty guys in the parking lot with their cars circled up, changing clothes in the middle every day. One of the parents even bought them milk crates with their names on them for lockers. We went 30–3 the rest of the way en route to a second championship in three years.

The Diving Play: In 2007, we were once again playing Faith Academy in the state championship. They had a hard-throwing right-hander, Justin Upchurch, on the mound. He was drafted by the Chicago White Sox that year and was topping out at ninety-four that day, so I knew this was going to be a tight, defensive game that probably would be decided in the last inning on a squeeze bunt or something. Well, that's what you get for thinking. We had scored nine runs by the fifth inning; the harder he threw it, the harder we hit it. By the seventh inning, we had twelve runs, but we couldn't seem to slow them down either. They had bases loaded in the last inning, with two outs, and our shortstop made one of the best plays I have ever seen. It's kind of hard to explain, but the batter hit a soft line drive toward left field, and Austin Allison came out of nowhere, it seemed, with a full extension dive toward the left fielder and made the catch. Honestly, I think it saved the game because they had so much momentum, and if that fell in, who knows what might have happened. I think what also made it so memorable for me is that he did the same thing in the quarter finals with the bases loaded on a ball hit up the middle that saved the game and allowed us to advance.

Drag Bunt with Big Murph: In the same series in 2007, after surviving a slugfest in game 1, we were locked up in pitcher's duel. We had one of the best pitchers in program history, Nathan Kilcrease, on the mound, so I wasn't very concerned about them scoring much, but they had a lefty that was carving us up. About halfway through the game, I could tell he had our number, and we would have to scratch and claw for whatever we could get. I have always been known as a small ball coach who takes pride in pitching and defense. However, the 2007 team probably had the most power of any team I have ever coached. We had several guys who could launch them into the trees, and after we hit the ball so well in the first game, conventional wisdom may have been to wait for one of them to hit one off the wall; but I just knew that wasn't going to happen. We had finally managed to get a couple guys on with a walk and error, so we had first and second with no outs. In stepped Tyler Murphy, standing six foot four and two hundred and fifty pounds. He could hit balls farther than any kid I've ever coached. He was actually a First Team All-American in junior college. So, of course, you know what happened then: drag bunt! They never even made a throw on the play, and now we had bases loaded, no outs, and were losing 2–0. Two hits later, we had a 4–2 lead and finished off the state championship series.

Pop Fly: We were playing one of the top-ranked 5A teams in the state of Florida at the end of our yearly spring break trip. Up by one run, with two outs, and runners on second and third. There's a pop fly to our first baseman, Dudley Taylor. It hits right in the palm of the glove and falls to the ground. We lost by one. Dudley was one of the best first baseman I have ever coached and one of the best leaders in program history, so to say he was devastated would be a huge understatement. As a coach, your heart truly breaks for the kid, but in these types of situations, you have to find words that will cauterize that wound so it doesn't fester. We didn't lose but one game the second half of the year in route to the 2009 State Championship.

Throw to Leftfield: Let me set this stage for you. It's the deciding game 3 of the state championship in 2009. We have already played two epic one-run games decided in the last inning. We are ahead by one in the seventh inning, with a runner on second base, and the batter has two strikes. I call time to meet with our pitcher and catcher. The message is clear and concise: "Don't worry about the runner at second base. He is the fastest guy in our association, and we could care less if he steals third base. Just get the batter!" What do you know, with the next pitch, he steals third and our catcher throws it into left field so the game is tied and goes into extra innings.

Not Coming Out: I told you a story from that epic 2009 three-game series in the state championship and how it went into extra innings, but what I didn't tell you was that the starting pitcher, Jacob Livingston, threw 138 pitches to secure that final game. I have always taken pride in not overusing pitchers, and through the years, I have always been very careful with pitch counts to put the player's arm health first, ahead of winning. Unfortunately all programs don't adhere to this and guys get hurt or, at the very least, wear down at the end of the season. After going to the eighth inning, he threw a few pitches and I could tell Jacob was exhausted. So I went for my last visit to the mound, and I will never forget what he told me. "Coach, I am never going to pitch again. Please let me finish this for you!" Three up, three down and the seventeenth championship in program history was in the books.

Seventeen Pitch At Bat: In 2010, we had a very inexperienced team. We graduated a lot of players from the previous year's club, so we were definitely the underdogs entering the state championship series. The team we were playing, Pike Liberal Arts, had only lost one game all season. They had their ace on the mound, and he was really good. We were young but very talented, and I felt if we could find a way to beat them in game 1 with their best guy out there, that momentum could carry us through the series. We were down 2–0 in the sixth inning, just like 2007, and believe me, those flashbacks were very vivid in my mind. This time we scratched two walks, and in stepped Spencer Riley—not what you would classify as an offensive juggernaut like Tyler Murphy. Spencer was one of the best defensive first baseman I've ever coached, and a scrappy hitter, but I knew he would have a tough time against this guy. To be honest, I don't know why I didn't bunt him, but he walked the first two guys, and Spencer had done a good job all year hitting behind runners, so I let him swing away. What followed was an epic battle of wills at historic Patterson Field in Montgomery, Alabama. He worked the count full, and pitch after pitch after pitch: foul ball, foul ball, foul ball. On the seventeenth pitch of the at-bat, he hit a ground ball with eyes, as we call them, and it somehow found its way between the outstretched arms of the shortstop and third baseman. We scored a run to pull within one, and they pulled the starting pitcher. The reliever was greeted with three straight hits, and we won the game 4–2. We won game 2, 6–5, fittingly ending on a pop-up to our catcher, Keaton Aldridge, to secure back-to-back state titles. I am fully convinced the momentum from that moment carried over. That young team realized they could beat anybody on any given day.

Our Rival: Those words tend to carry a lot of weight when it comes to athletic competition. Now if you ask most coaches, this is more for the fans, newspapers, and television than the people on the field actually competing; but nevertheless, it has its place in every community around the country. Each sport can have a different rival depending on what programs are competing at a high level for a few years. Really close games for several years in a row with a certain school or even some trash-talking within the community can earn that classification. However, most schools have a natural rivalry, and it's usually determined by geographic location and competition over the same state athletic titles. That rival for us is Lee-Scott Academy in Auburn, Alabama. Now since I've been the head coach, my record against them is 31–5, so we have definitely had the upper hand on the field. But every time we play, the stands are full and it's a big deal for our communities. Now, I have always had great relationships with their coaches and respect their players immensely, but in 2011, we hosted our rival for the state semifinals, and it was nuts! We had to bring all the bleachers from the softball field for extra seating, and it was still standing-room only. The atmosphere was definitely different from a regular season series, as it should have been with a berth to the state championship on the line. Well, our boys were ready to the tune of twenty-seven runs in two lopsided victories. This was highlighted by our leadoff hitter, Will Allison, going 8–9 in the doubleheader, including hitting for the cycle (HR, 3B, 2B, 1B) in game 2. It was an amazing night!

Packed Stadium: After that amazing night in front of our home crowd in the semifinals, we found ourselves in a familiar position against Pike Liberal Arts in the state finals for the second consecutive year. However, there was one major difference: the games were at night! For some reason, unbeknownst to me, our state championship has always been during the middle of the day, making it tough for fans to get to a neutral site without taking off from work. This year was different, and man, was it awesome. I remember looking into the stands during the third inning of the first game, and it was packed. Usually as a general rule when coaching, you don't really notice the crowd because you are so wrapped up in trying to win on the field, but this atmosphere definitely caught my attention. Our student section was rocking, and you could feel the electricity. We lost the first game of the doubleheader, but that didn't take one ounce of enthusiasm from our fans. The second game was an 11–1 victory, but to be honest, I don't remember many details about the game, only the amazing crowd!

Fifty-Nine Pitch Complete Game: After the dust settled from an emotional night and the packed stadium, all focus was on a deciding game 3 for the 2011 State Championship. Throughout my career, I have always tried to develop a pitcher during the season that the teams we might meet in the state championship would know little or nothing about. Often it's a young guy, but sometimes it's just a guy I never throw in region games or even in our state for that matter. I do make sure that whoever this pitcher is, he has pitched against good competition the entire year so he is not overwhelmed by the situation. That year is was Tyler Condrey, and Pike didn't know what hit them. He was a finesse pitcher who pounded the strike zone and could pitch backward. We threw breaking balls in fastball counts and vice versa. Pop up after pop up after pop up, and his only strikeout came on the last pitch of the game, his fifty-ninth! He dropped down and threw a side-armed curveball that he had not thrown in a game all year—only during our bullpen sessions. What a moment to have the courage to do that on the biggest stage of his life.

Shot Heard Around the World: In 2014, we faced a familiar foe, Monroe Academy, in the state semifinals at home. It was a deciding game 3 after an epic thirteen-inning, 1–0 loss the night before. Our place was packed, all the stands were full, and it was standing-room only down the sidelines. We are losing 6–2 in the bottom of the seventh inning. We managed to get the bases loaded, but there were two outs, and in stepped Chad Silvani. His older brother, Chase, was part of two state championship teams in 2010 and 2011 and was playing D1 baseball at the time. I only tell you that to help people understand the pressure some brothers may feel in our program when they have not won a championship and their brother has. That being said, Chad was a great player for us and had gotten big hits over the years in clutch situations, so why not now? He knew walking to the plate he would have to hit an off-speed pitch. He stood about six foot five and two hundred and forty pounds, so he was a pretty imposing young man. The bases were loaded with the season on the line. That's what I would throw him: curveball for strike one, curveball for strike two. Chad stepped out, took a deep breath, and crushed the next curveball over the lights in right centerfield to tie the game. The place went nuts, and we found out later one of the middle school kids watching the game from the bullpen recorded it. It instantly went viral, and the legend of Chad Silvani in Glenwood Baseball lure was born. Wouldn't you know, he came up with the bases loaded the very next inning and got walked on four straight? No way were they going to pitch to him again!

During my time as a coach, there are not only memories from specific games that are stand-out individual performances, but often they are thoughts that span over several years and are strictly about the team and program as a whole. These I've chosen to share because when I reflect on them, they make me extremely proud to call myself a coach and are why I encourage as many people as possible to serve something bigger than themselves.

Gator Valley: Very rarely do I use conditioning as punishment; however, over the years, there have been a few epic journeys to Gator Valley. This valley sits about a quarter mile behind our baseball field and has become a source of pride for some and agony for others. From time to time, teams need a wake-up call when they get comfortable, and it's the perfect place for it. Not only is it a 45-degree incline, it's over fifty yards long, and the years have not been kind to the ol' girl. Weather and erosion have given it many different facelifts, and sometimes choosing your route is the most important decision of the day for a baseball player. One of the most commonly asked questions from former players is, "Coach, when is the last time you took them to Gator Valley?"

Mighty Faith Academy: Early in my career, there was definitely one coach who stood out to me: Lloyd Skoda from Faith Academy in Mobile, Alabama. His teams were always very talented, but what I loved about his teams were how disciplined and fundamentally sound they were. We had some great games over the years, which included battles with reigning MLB American League MVP, Josh Donaldson. Most of the time they were tight games that were well pitched and featured outstanding defensive plays. He was so humble despite being a legend, and gracious in victory as well as defeat. He always made time for me, not only when we played each other but at the state and national conventions. Despite winning multiple state championships and coaching several Major League players, I always saw him taking notes at clinics, talking to other coaches about the game, and being willing to share any of his knowledge with young coaches. I have told him this before, but I can never thank him enough for setting that kind of example for me follow. No matter how successful you are, you are never bigger than the game. As a coach, I was privileged to win my first two state championships against one of the greatest high school coaches ever, but more important to me, against a great man and mentor.

College Games: I love taking our team to college games. More times than not, it is to watch one of our former players, and we usually do this around our scheduled road trips when it's feasible. They not only get to maybe see a former Glenwood Gator they look up to, but they gain a greater appreciation for what it takes to get to the next level and how the speed of the game changes. It is also another way to let college coaches know you run a first-class program and are serious about getting your guys to college.

Community Service: I have such great memories over the years from events we have done in our community and even communities around the world. We have volunteered at homeless shelters, done grounds maintenance for battered women's shelters, helped with disaster relief efforts, worked with the child advocacy center, and even helped build a home on *Extreme Makeover Home Edition*. Each and every time, I have been so proud to be a part of any effort to make our community better, but selfishly being with my guys while doing it brings a level of joy I can't truly explain in words. When you actually witness, with your own two eyes, a noticeable change in a young man's perspective on life, it humbles you beyond belief. Seeing young men in other countries being put in uncomfortable situations and figuring out how to become comfortable gives me hope for a new generation of servants that understand the importance of putting others ahead of themselves.

End of Year Speeches: If you ask any coach, one of the hardest things in the world is knowing what to say on the field to the players when that last game is played and their season is over. When that finality hits the seniors square in the mouth and something they have poured so much of their life into is gone, it can be a very emotional time. Fortunately for us, we've won our last game several times, so it does make it a little easier to bear when everyone has tears of joy from finishing on top. Even then, I think it is extremely important to choose your words wisely when addressing your team because you will never get that moment back to make a lasting impression. For the most part, I feel your words need to be positive in nature but, above all else, honest. Through the years, I have always thanked our kids for their service to our program, their dedication, and what they mean to me as a person. However, there was one season when I called out the seniors for their lack of leadership and selfishness because I felt it was, without a doubt, necessary for them going forward as young men. I am happy to say that to this day, I am as close to some of those players as any I have ever coached. There is one quote I specifically remember telling a team after we lost a tough three-game series in the state semifinals: "Baseball does not define who you are; it teaches you the man you can become!"

Banquets: End-of-the-year ceremonies are done differently everywhere you go. Some have dinner, some give out individual awards and certificates, but what all of them have in common is recognizing student-athletes for their achievements on the field. I have always felt it's important for the parents to see a side of you they wouldn't normally see. For the most part, they observe you at games in the heat of athletic competition and not on a daily basis at practice, community service projects, and team functions, when your true relationship is developed with their children. Now I am not really a proponent of individual awards; I am more in favor of senior and team awards, but I do always talk about the players and their contributions to the program. It is also imperative that you recognize the sacrifice parents make year after year for your program to be successful, and certainly never forget to thank your wife! When talking about your players, it's okay to get emotional because that's real. Trying to hide that doesn't paint a true picture of who you are, and man, over the years, we have had some tearjerkers. One of the greatest compliments I have ever received as a coach came at one of my former players' weddings. During his dad's speech, he thanked me for teaching him it was okay to cry in front of people.

Former Players: I have been blessed to coach so many great players over the years, and I will tell you that no one player has been any more important than the others. Of course, from the outside looking in, it would be easy to assume coaches have a closer relationship with guys who were All-Americans, got drafted, or went on to have great college careers, but that is just not the case. I have always maintained that the guy just fighting to get a shot to play college baseball is just as important as the D1 prospect; and equally as important is the guy who has been in our program fighting tooth and nail just to make the team and be a contributor. They are all important for so many reasons, but first and foremost because they serve something greater than themselves. My former players come to visit me all the time, and never once do I think about where they hit in the lineup, how many games they won on the mound, if they were All-State or if they sat the bench—only that I love each and every one of them. No matter how beautiful we make our facilities or how many state championships we win, that will never change.

This is a text I received from one of my players, Brandon Moseley, "You managed to be the missing piece to the puzzle in a lot of aspects in my life. It's never just been about baseball. I came here and was given a chance, but you took the game of life to a completely different level for me. I'm not done and try to grow every day, but you were essential in my life for the last four years and it really does mean a lot to me. You were never scared to jump on my case when I acted dumb or was irresponsible and I respect that more than you know. I love you coach and I really do appreciate everything you have done for me." Now that's why I coach and that's why it's *More Than A Game*!

Judge yourself as a coach by how many former players come to see you!

CHAPTER 10

Humble Beginnings

I have shared small glimpses of my life with you throughout this book; however, I feel it's important to share with you more about my life growing up. My mother was born in Foxboro, Massachusetts. Her father was a farmer, and her mother was a homemaker. She had five siblings and was raised in the Roman Catholic Church. Just a hard-working Italian family from New England that, like a lot of families from that era, valued hard work, family, and faith above everything else. After high school, Mom went to school to become a nurse. At age twenty-seven, she joined the army during the end of the Vietnam War. After basic training, she was stationed in Fort Benning, Georgia.

While stationed there, she became pregnant with me and had a choice to make. Back then, single mothers were not allowed to stay in the army if they didn't have someone to sign as a legal guardian, so it was either give me up for adoption or keep me and be honorably discharged from the service. Not to mention by choosing to have me out of wedlock, it certainly would cause a great deal of tension with her family back home and their strong religious ideas about marriage. Luckily for me, all she cared about was being blessed with her first child, and the rest of it didn't matter to her. It was a struggle for Mom from that point forward. There was a failed marriage five years later that blessed us with my sister, Charlene. This was followed by another failed long-time relationship five years later that blessed us with my youngest sister, Jennifer. Now if you ask her, she wouldn't have it any other way.

When Mom discharged from the army, she was a registered nurse, so she thought finding a job wouldn't be that difficult. Well, she was right, but all the jobs she found were third shift, and that was not a legitimate option as a single mother with no one to watch your child. This began a long list of dead-end jobs that didn't pay well, and she had no career path. She took whatever job she could, and most of the time had two or three jobs to make ends meet. She worked at the grounds department for the local university and a t-shirt printing shop, cleaned houses and landscaped yards. During a ten-year period in which my sisters and I came along, she tried to go back to school on the GI Bill, but it was just too hard for her to raise three kids, work multiple jobs, and do her school work. We moved a lot, and I never really felt settled until I was about ten years old. That's when I believe God really stepped in and began to show my mom the path for our family.

You have to understand, by this time I had already been exposed to alcoholism, physical and verbal abuse, and even sexual molestation. The neighborhoods—or I should say trailer parks—we lived in on the south side of Columbus were full of drugs and gangs. My mother was doing the best she could, but the environment we were living in was a train wreck. When you see and experience these things at a young age, you start to become hardened, and if you aren't careful, you accept this as normal.

Just before I turned ten, Mom found a very small two-bedroom house on the east side of town. It had not been painted in probably twenty years and had holes in the walls, but it was a house and not a trailer. It had a yard and not a barbed wire fence next to a junkyard. It was directly across the street from Eastern Little League and walking distance from East Columbus Boy's Club and Edgewood Elementary School.

When I talked to my mother about this time in our lives, her response was simple: "I have asked forgiveness for mistakes as a parent many times, and during that, soon realized with God's help and unconditional love for my children, anything is and will always be possible while serving at the right hand of the Father." As she said those words to me, I thought about myself as a parent and the mistakes we all make when trying to raise our children. Everyone, by nature, wants to provide more for their children than what they had growing up, but I believe that's where most of our mistakes begin. When we focus on providing materialistic things, we lose sight of the fact that we are not in control. Our job as parents is to provide a loving environment, encouragement, and teach our children right from wrong. Most important, we must show them that God has a path for all of us.

When I look back on my life to this point, that time period always seems so crucial to how my life has turned out and the journey I have been on ever since. I mentioned earlier the impact being introduced to my first male role model had on me while playing Little League baseball. What I didn't mention was the impact Butch Sanford, the director of the Boy's Club, had on me.

Not only was the Boy's Club like a second home to me, it introduced me to so many different things. I had never swum before or tried pottery, art, ping-pong, or bumper pool. These things seem very trivial now as an adult, but growing up where I did, they were so extraordinary. It really opened my eyes to a world I didn't know existed. I remember Butch really showing an interest in me, and whether he knows it or not, he demonstrated several leadership qualities that would certainly help me for many years to come. When raised by a single mother, there is a lot of alone time after school. We didn't have cable or air-conditioning, so I certainly wasn't going to stay in the house, and I am sure the Boy's and Girl's Clubs are that place for thousands across America. I would hate to think what I might have gotten into if I didn't have that place to go to.

Growing up, I don't ever remember resenting people for having materialistic things I knew I would never have. We were on food stamps and received free lunches at school, but that was just normal. It wasn't uncommon for me to come home to find another family living with us because they had nowhere else to go and my mother couldn't say no. In high school, we moved to the north side of town, to a bigger house. Only two small space heaters made it interesting in the winter, and I do remember my mother falling through the floor while in the bathtub one time. When I moved away to college, my mother was selected for a new house from Habitat for Humanity. The location was back on the south side, not far from where my life began, so it was a high crime area; but nevertheless, it was really cool to see her receive such a blessing and the feeling of pride she carried to finally have something of her own. She has been there almost twenty-five years now.

I do think these things motivated me to stay focused on what I wanted in life. I will tell you that one of my favorite shows on television was *Lifestyles of the Rich and Famous*. I can still remember the host, Robin Leach's, voice to this day. Just because I didn't resent not having fancy cars and mansions in exotic locations, doesn't mean I wasn't a dreamer. Now, of course, as I have gotten older and God's path has been laid out for me, I understand these things are not what will ultimately make me happy. I understand that happiness is relative to the manner of life you lead and your perspective on every day that you are blessed with breath in your lungs. I have seen kids living in extreme poverty with just as big a smiles as Hollywood actors on the red carpet at the Oscars!

In my life, for example, I never felt bitter that we didn't have air-conditioning, central heat, or cable television. I think it gave me a greater appreciation for those things later in life. When I got to college and added three meals a day on top of that, I didn't think it could possibly get any better! I might as well have been living in Beverly Hills or the Hamptons. Sure, there was no spending money or a mode of transportation, but I just adapted and made it work. I never had those things before. I guess you don't miss what you never had in the first place.

The only time I came home was when I could convince one of my teammates to come stay with me for a few days. I will admit, seeing the look on my friends' faces when there was a drug march in the neighborhood or two crackheads in my front yard was priceless. Knowing what I know now, that was an invaluable experience for those guys to see a part of society they had only heard about or seen on television but never experienced for themselves. I always knew growing up how to evaluate true friendships without fail. If they came to my house and still wanted to hang out again, they were keepers. You never know how someone is going to react to roaches, wharf rats, and a less than stellar selection of creature comforts. That goes for girls as well. My wife passed that test with flying colors. Now I will say it didn't hurt my feelings any when they invited me to come stay the weekend with them either. Sliding away from reality for a brief moment is not always a bad thing as long as it doesn't last too long!

After reading Malcolm Gladwell's *Outliers,* I really began to question why and how I've become who I am today. He explains understanding successful people and how we have come to focus too much on their intelligence, ambition, and personality traits when we should focus on the world that surrounds them, including their culture, their family, their generation, and the experiences of their upbringing. As I was reading, I found myself searching for answers as to why I have been so blessed with success professionally and personally despite my circumstances growing up. Some way or another, we always had food on the table, a roof over our heads, and clothes on our backs despite the fact that the family finances showed that as being impossible. If we had never moved down the street from the Boy's Club and across from Eastern Little League, would I have ever played sports? Would I have gone on to play college and professional baseball and received a free college education? Did growing up in these communities give me an overwhelming desire to travel around the world, serving others? However, the more I thought about it, the one outlier that was missing for me was God's path.

I believe everyone in this world has an opportunity to be successful, regardless of their outliers, but so often our ideas of success are tainted by the world's definition of it, not our own. Only your effort and your heart can change your circumstances. Never look to others for true fulfillment, but look inward so that your joy can be shared with everyone you may come in contact with, in hopes of igniting inspiration that will last for generations to come!

CHAPTER 11

Dirt Road

All great leaders need their dirt road. This is the road less traveled where so many life-changing decisions are made. Unlike the nice paved roads that are clearly marked and have turning lanes, this road often has no signs. It doesn't have a traffic light with a green arrow pointing you in the right direction. Instead, it has uncertainty, self-doubt, and second-guessing. Not to mention the potholes, rocks, and dust that make it very difficult to navigate. What it does have is a purpose! The easy thing to do is follow the crowd at chow time and be the status quo! God has given all of us the ability to be so much more than that. Everyone has the ability to lead by serving others, but it's only by getting rid of the world's perception of you. Leaders do not care about what other people think of them because they serve something bigger than themselves.

There are so many parallels when it comes to athletics and our walk with Christ. As coaches, we work so hard to get to the top, and any successful coach will tell you the same thing: getting to the top is the easy part; staying at the top is what separates a great team from a great program! I think the same is true of our faith. The easy part is to accept Christ as your savior after a great sermon and altar call or even in a small group where you feel comfortable confessing your sins and asking forgiveness. The hard part, when the dust settles, is your daily walk. When you look yourself in the mirror and have to ask, "What have I done to further his kingdom today?" If you have played sports at a competitive level, I am quite sure you have had a coach or two tell you to go home and look yourself in the mirror and ask a very simple question: "Am I doing everything I can?"

The same is true with God. Are we working hard at it every day or just when it's convenient? Are we only praying during times of crisis or truly delving into the word? Are we sharing with others and, most important, with our own families? If you are an athlete and only train when you are told to or when you think it's expected, you will never achieve ultimate success, on or off the field. So why should it be any different in your spirituality? Well it's not! The leaders we all aspire to be, no matter the profession, all have one thing in common: their path. They find it, commit to it, and stay on it! No matter the obstacles, outside expectations, setbacks, negativity, or how winding the path maybe, that dirt road is theirs and theirs alone. "Blessed is a man who endures trials, because when he passes the test he will receive the crown of life that He has promised to those that love him" (James 1:12 Holman Christian Standard Bible).

Caring what people think prevents you from reaching your potential as a human being!

.

Printed in the United States
By Bookmasters